ADDICTIVE DISORDERS UPDATE
Alcoholism/Drug Abuse/Gambling

ADDICTIVE DISORDERS
UPDATE
Alcoholism/Drug Abuse/Gambling

Edited by

Pasquale A. Carone, M.D.

South Oaks Hospital
Amityville, New York

Stanley F. Yolles, M.D.

State University of New York at Stony Brook
Stony Brook, New York

Sherman N. Kieffer, M.D.

State University of New York at Stony Brook
Stony Brook, New York

Leonard W. Krinsky, Ph.D.

South Oaks Hospital
Amityville, New York

HV5035
A33
1982

Volume VII in the Series
Problems of Industrial Psychiatric Medicine

Series Editor: Sherman N. Kieffer, M.D.

 **HUMAN SCIENCES PRESS, INC.**
72 Fifth Avenue   3 Henrietta Street
NEW YORK, NY 10011 ● LONDON, WC2E 8LU

Library of Congress Catalog Number 78-23720

ISBN: 0-87705-389-8

Copyright © 1982 by Human Sciences Press, Inc.
72 Fifth Avenue, New York, New York 10011

Printed in the United States of America
0123456789 987654

Library of Congress Cataloging in Publication Data

Addictive disorders update.

(Problems of industrial psychiatric medicine; v. 7)
Includes index.
1.Alchoholism—Addresses, essays, lectures.
2. Drug abuse—Addresses, essays, lectures.   3. Gambling
—Addresses, essays, lectures. I. Carone, Pasquale A.
II. Series.
HV5035.A33   362.2'9   81-6880
ISBN 0-89885-034-7   AACR2

CONTENTS

CONTRIBUTORS

LUTHER A. CLOUD, M.D.
Board Member
National Council on Alcoholism, Inc.

ROBERT L. CUSTER, M.D.
Chief of Treatment Division
Mental Health Services
Veterans Administration Central Office

ROBERT M. DERMAN, M.D.
Chief, Psychiatry Service
Veterans Administration Hospital

Associate Professor of Psychiatry
Department of Psychiatry and Behavioral Science
School of Medicine
Health Sciences Center
State University of New York at Stony Brook

WALTER DONHEISER, Ph.D.
Coordinator
Drug Abuse Programs
South Oaks Hospital

REV. MSGR. JOSEPH A. DUNNE
President, Executive Director
The National Council on Compulsive Gambling, Inc.

ROBERT L. DuPONT, M.D.
Founding Director
National Institute on Drug Abuse
President
Institute for Behavior and Health, Inc.

LEON D. HANKOFF, M.D.
Professor of Psychiatry
Department of Psychiatry and Behavioral Science
School of Medicine
Health Sciences Center
State University of New York at Stony Brook

SHERMAN N. KIEFFER, M.D.
Professor and Vice-Chairman
Department of Psychiatry and Behavioral Science
School of Medicine
Health Sciences Center
State University of New York at Stony Brook

ALEXANDER J. LICASTRO, M.D.
Family Practitioner

HERBERT MARTEY, M.A.
Director of Alcoholism Programs
South Oaks Hospital

THADDEUS J. MURAWSKI, M.D.
Director
Office of Professional Medical Conduct
State of New York Department of Health

WAYNE ROTHWELL, C.S.W.
Director
Drug Abuse Programs
South Oaks Hospital

REV. PETER SWEISGOOD, O.S.B.
Assistant Executive Director
Long Island Council on Alcoholism

THREE MEMBERS OF GAMBLERS ANONYMOUS

MAXWELL N. WEISMAN, M.D.
Director
Alcoholism Control Administration
Department of Health and Mental Hygiene
State of Maryland

RICHARD ZOPPA, M.D.
Senior Psychiatrist
South Oaks Hospital

PREFACE

On April 5th and 6th, 1979, South Oaks Foundation, in conjunction with the Department of Psychiatry, Health Sciences Center, State University of New York at Stony Brook, sponsored a conference entitled "Update on Addictive Disorders."

Our joint concern with substance abuse dates back many years. Our first conference in 1971 was entitled "Alcoholism in Industry" and our second was "Drug Abuse in Industry." All in the mental health professions, as well as management and labor, have been deeply concerned for many years as to the disastrous effects of substance abuse. Industry and labor are deeply concerned over absenteeism, job accidents, losses of jobs, and their overall costs. They, in addition to the health professions, are also deeply concerned from a more humanitarian standpoint with what substance abuse does, not only to the individual but to the entire family and to the community.

This volume is one in which those with varying viewpoints have an opportunity to come together for a synthesis of opinions. Our keynote speakers and panelists included not only those who would speak on the common substance abuses, such as alcohol and drugs, but we also included representatives from Gamblers Anonymous.

The results of the conference are not surprising. Much has been accomplished in the field over the past several years but the consensus was that much remains to be done. The two-day conference at South Oaks Hospital set the stage for further considerations and further discussions. It also was of great benefit in again bringing together representatives of various, diverse groups so that a common denominator for working together could be established.

INTRODUCTION

Questions that must be answered are why can most people drink in moderation, gamble sensibly, and take medicine solely for health reasons while others cannot; why do certain people satisfy needs by gambling to excess or drinking to excess or by becoming addicted to drugs and why do certain people seek one outlet and others another.

Pasquale A. Carone, M.D.

This book is concerned with the various addictive disorders—alcoholism, drug abuse, and compulsive gambling. It approaches these problems in diverse and yet related ways. Keynote speakers included not only the health professionals, but also members of self-help groups who suffer from addictive disorders and are struggling to overcome them. All, however, agree as to the destruction of personality that is a by-product of the addictive disorders. This not only involves the individual concerned but the nuclear and extended family as well as the community. It is also extremely costly in terms of money with losses of jobs, absenteeism, job accidents, thefts, embezzlements, etc., that come about because of substance abuse.

The thrust of the conference was in part to demythologize the health professional while emphasizing that addictive disorders represent a disease, a disease with its own ideology, genealogy, prodromata, and onset. While our various speakers disagree in many areas, all are in unanimous agreement as to the value of AA and other self-help approaches.

The reader may be surprised by the statistics regarding narcotics addiction and habituation. It is impossible to go through this book without noting that there is almost a hierarchical structure in regard to substance abuse with the alcoholics on top and drug users on the bottom. There is increasing recognition that alcoholism is an illness, but there is still a tendency to treat the drug user as a pariah. There is emphasis on the therapeutic value of self-help groups, but concomitantly there are legal strictures regarding drug use as compared to alcohol.

Our speakers included a health professional who has specialized in the treatment of compulsive gamblers. In addition the conference was addressed by three compulsive gamblers who are meeting varying degrees of success in combating their compulsion. It is our belief that this presentation, as presented in this book, is one of the best organized and substantive overviews of the problem that is available. There is emphasis on the fact that gambling can be a pleasurable challenge for much of the population but represents a pathologic disorder to a relatively small group. The reader will be impressed with the growth of Gamblers Anonymous and the positive force it has been in the treatment of compulsive gambling. There is also emphasis on the psychiatric aspects of the disorder particularly on the need to see the compulsive gambler as a potential suicidal threat.

There was a dual purpose to this conference: to educate and establish lines of communication. It is our hope that not only the participant but also the reader will be introduced to new ideas and new concepts. A continuing dialogue in regard to substance abuse is essential.

ACKNOWLEDGMENTS

This book is one of a continuing series dedicated to various aspects of psychiatric industrial medicine. Each year South Oaks Hospital and the State University of New York at Stony Brook co-sponsor these conferences. These are held in the spring of each year and in the past have addressed themselves to such topics as "Alcoholism in Industry," "Drug Abuse in Industry," "Absenteeism in Industry," etc.

This book represents a distillation of the most important parts of the keynote speeches and the panel discussions that follow. The book would not be possible without the active cooperation of all the keynote speakers and panelists.

We are also indebted to the Board of Directors of South Oaks Hospital who have been most kind in supporting these annual conferences since 1971.

We are also deeply indebted to our Executive Assistant, Catherine Martens, and our Director of Community Relations, Lynn Black.

Chapter 1

ALCOHOLISM IN INDUSTRY—THE THREAT AND THE PROMISE

Maxwell N. Weisman, M.D.*

I stand here in amazement as I see the number of people who are gathered to discuss this subject, which, when announced in other places, becomes conspicuous by the paucity of the people who attend. I am, therefore, somewhat overwhelmed because I didn't expect this crowd.

The title is intriguing but presents an almost insuperable challenge since it is difficult to know how to approach this two-pronged subject of the threat and the promise of alcoholism. I prefer not to go into detail on the threat of alcoholism to the alcoholic individual. I am sure a

*Maxwell N. Weisman received his M.D. at the University of Amsterdam in 1958, returning to this country for further training at the Psychiatric Institute in Baltimore. In 1962 he joined the Maryland Department of Mental Hygiene as Director of Community Psychiatry and, in 1968, was appointed the first Director of the State's Alcoholism Control Administration of which he is now the Medical Director. He is a Diplomate of the American Board of Psychiatry and Neurology in Psychiatry and a Fellow of the American Psychiatric Association. He is on the teaching faculty of the Johns Hopkins and the University of Maryland Medical Schools, the author of numerous papers on community psychiatry, psychoanalysis, and alcoholism, and a popular lecturer at national and international meetings.

sophisticated audience is only too familiar with the havoc that alcoholism creates—the wasted lives, the broken homes, the effects on one's health from the central nervous system to every organ system of the body, the crime rate, the driving while intoxicated, and the deaths on the highways. The economics of the effect of alcoholism on the individual and the subsequent effect on our national economy are staggering. I am sure you have heard before about absenteeism, accident rates in industry, bad decisions, and the half-men and half-women present at work. So I am going to eschew that kind of presentation, as I think there are other aspects that have not really been considered in as great detail as they deserve.

I'd like to talk about the threat to alcoholism *programs*. I submit there are two major threats. One is that of ignorance. Now we know that alcoholism has been defined as a disease by the American Medical Association and by many state legislatures. As a matter of fact, Maryland, the state I adopted, happens to have been the first to declare that alcoholism is a disease and that public intoxication is simply a symptom of that disease and therefore no longer subject to the criminal justice system. Since then, some thirty-odd states have followed suit. As a result of acknowledging the disease aspect of alcoholism, many physicians have been drawn into the treatment process. But the great bulk of American physicians are ignorant about alcoholism because they have not been trained to treat this disease that continues to sweep this country. Also, a great many doctors have little humility when it comes to working in this field. One of my colleagues has said that every doctor who gets an M.D. degree also acquires an M.D.-ity, and that is an unfortunate phenomenon when you work with alcoholics. In medical school, I never heard a lecturer say that when I got my degree, I'd become God. I never read it in a medical textbook either, but it is very easy to read between the lines. I notice some of you are snickering; don't laugh, it is true not only of the medical profession, it is true of social workers, nurses, and the clergy—perhaps the clergy have more of a right to this attitude, but it is curtains if you work with alcoholics, unless you have really learned some humility.

It was difficult for me when I first started working with alcoholics to acquire this deep-seated sense of humility that is so necessary. I remember one of my first patients when I hung my shingle out as a psychiatrist. He brought in his wife and he was very unhappy. He had taken a few drinks that day in order to fortify himself with enough courage to see me. I spent more than an hour with him that first session and laid on the line what I had learned about alcoholism by attending AA meetings and by reading some of the literature. I acquainted him with the idea that it was a disease and that we needed to establish a contract where he would verbalize his deep underlying conflicts and I would listen and attempt to make appropriate intrepretations, so that he could learn how to cope with these conflicts that had been unresolved.

He looked at me and said, "Doctor, you are marvelous. Nobody had ever told me before that I was suffering from a disease. My wife thinks I am a weakling. She pours the booze down the sink so I just have to get some more booze. My employer has fired me, time and again. You're the first one who is treating me with some respect and understanding of my condition."

When I told him that he needed to stay sober in order to be in psychotherapy, that he needed to go to AA in order to help him to stay sober, he promised to do all these things and with shining eyes he left me, eager to come back the following Monday for his first real therapy hour.

Well, I walked into the bathroom to wash my hands and I looked at myself in the mirror, and ladies and gentlemen, my eyes were glowing just as much as his. I looked at myself and said, "Max, you really are a great doctor. It is easy to work with alcoholics. You just have to level with them and help them." I couldn't wait, myself, until the next Monday night when he would come in and we would start working on who stole his little red wagon when he was three, and there he was Monday night, bombed! I kept this up because I thought I had not reached him and it was week after week of a lack of success. Well, as I say, nobody had told me I was God but I felt that I was failing with this man. After a number of weeks, what did I tend to do? I had a tendency to say, "Joe, you are not motivated. Come back and see me when you are ready to stop drinking." What nonsense! It was I who was not motivated to treat him. Because with M.D.-ity I couldn't face a sense of failure. God doesn't fail, by definition, and so you tend to reject your alcoholic patients. Fortunately I had some good supervision and I listened a little more carefully at AA meetings.

I remember the first meeting I went to, after I was so frustrated in the emergency room of the hospital where I did a rotating internship. When I suggested that patients go to AA because that fellowship was good for people like them, the answer each one gave to me was, "Why, that is for those alcoholics. I'm not an alcoholic." Yet each one of them had been coming in from the Skid Row area almost night after night because they were hurting and they needed some help. I finally went to my first AA meeting in desperation to find out what pearls of wisdom they were dropping so I could learn from them. I was still in my white uniform because I had just come off duty. When I got to the church, several meetings were in progress and I couldn't tell which one was the AA meeting. I went from one doorway to another and they all looked alike. They could have been Bible classes for all I knew. But in one of them the meeting hadn't quite started; there was a coffee urn in the corner and there were a few men around it. One of them noticed me hesitating in the doorway. He walked over and said, "Are you looking for AA?" With a sigh of relief, I said, "Yes, thank you." He said, "Come on in, you're welcome, are you an alcoholic?" I said, "No, I am not." Then he looked at me kind of funny and I realized that that is what all my patients had been telling *me*. Maybe I was and I'd better start listening carefully.

Well, I am not talking about the people with no humility, either, or the bad doctors. I am talking about the bulk of the American medical profession who are excellent doctors and yet they have never been trained in medical school up until just a few years ago (and even then it is just a drop in the bucket) about this dread disease.

In Maryland in 1968 a law was passed declaring that police must pick up an alcoholic who is incapacitated and if he has no home to go to, they must take him to the nearest emergency room. I toured one of the large hospitals where one of my colleagues was chief of medicine, and I asked him how many alcoholics had been admitted in the wards. He looked at me slyly and said, "Max, you know that we don't treat alcoholics; as soon as they are brought in by the police and they are diagnosed as alcoholics we ship them off to the state mental hospital." I said, "That's nonsense, you've been treating alcoholics in your wards for a long time and I'll bet you have them there right now." He said, "You are such a fanatic you see an alcoholic under every bed." Well, we went to the ward and picked 40 charts at random and leafed through them. I read the social histories and, lo and behold, I plucked out 16 of those 40 charts. I said, "These people, I think, are alcoholics." He was angry with me because not one of the excellent interns and residents and attending physicians had diagnosed alcoholism. It wasn't even mentioned in the history. There were the usual cases of diabetes and coronaries and fractures and everything else you can imagine. Yet, I thought 16 of them—40 percent of that first batch of 40—were alcoholics, and he wouldn't believe it. So we went to the bedsides and we interviewed each of these 16 patients. Of course I was taking my life in my hands because there was nothing in the social histories that described the drinking practices.

I remember one man who was a foreman at a large steel plant who was admitted with a third-degree burn. He was heavily bandaged when we got to his bedside. The story was that his wife had gone to visit her family during the weekend and he indulged in a practice that his wife had forbidden, smoking in bed. He told the intern that he had been watching television and had had a couple of beers and felt sleepy and sure enough the bed caught fire and he was admitted in a serious state. Well, any time I hear, "All I had was a couple of beers," I begin to be a little suspicious. My index goes up. Now you can't be sure, of course, because there is such a realistic phenomenon as two beers. But I took a chance and sat down with him and established rapport. I commiserated with him about his strict and dominating wife, and he felt that he had an ally. What came out in our discussion was that he had three DWI's (drinking while intoxicated). He had never volunteered that. The intern had never asked that kind of question. He did not think it was related to his burn. But there it was now. He had gotten into serious trouble because of his drinking and could have been recognized as an alcoholic. Unless you diagnose it, you don't treat it. The man would have been discharged, fully recovered from his burn, and left to go back to his old life style of a "couple of beers."

Another man was the vice-president in a large corporation. He was admitted with a compound fracture of the tibia-fibula and was in traction when we saw him. The social history, to me, was fascinating because here his drinking had been mentioned. He had attended an office Christmas party. He did become intoxicated, doesn't everybody? He even drove home. Successfully. His tolerance was apparently very high. He came into his mansion and tried to climb into the marriage bed, but his wife, smelling booze and seeing lipstick smeared all over him, rejected him. This man was so furious, he cussed his wife up and down and called her all sorts of names (all of which was in the social history) and then he said, "If you won't have me I'll go to the nearest whore." He put his trousers back on, unfortunately the wrong way around. He ran down his marble stairs and got caught in the suspenders, tripped, and broke his tibia-fibula.

That can happen to anybody after an office party! In our conversation it came out that he was thinking of divorcing his wife. He had also had two previous divorces from women who could not stand his drinking!

Well, both of these men, as you can see, were clearly alcoholics. I got away with the other 14 as well. My colleague was so appalled by the poor medicine that was being practiced in his hospital that he ran to the administrator and said, "I want to have a seminar on alcoholism." That was the first time he had an educational program in that hospital, specifically geared toward the study of alcoholism. So I am talking about excellent doctors who do some beautiful medicine but who are ignorant of alcoholism.

In addition to ignorance, there is another threat to an alcoholism program and that lies in the attitudes, not only on the part of the medical profession and other helping individuals, but of society at large. We in medicine, or in social work or psychology, or nursing, or even the clergy, simply reflect the social mores and customs and attitudes that we imbibe, without knowing, in our mother's milk. One of these attitudes, of course, is that there is something stigmatizing about being an alcoholic; the attitude that it is not really a disease. This, in spite of the announcements of the AMA, in spite of the extensive literature on alcoholism, and in spite of the criteria for the diagnosis of alcoholism as a disease as published by the Criteria Committee of the National Council on Alcoholism, way back in 1972! Two easily accessible journals, *The American Journal of Psychiatry* and *The Internal Medicine Journal*, also published the same article in August 1972. Yet it has not sunk deeply enough into the medical profession.

At a recent state medical society annual conference in the Bible Belt, I gave a banquet speech on alcoholism. I pointed out that alcoholism is not characteristic of everybody who drinks. I said there are roughly about 100 million adults in this country who drink alcohol. I asked, "Is there anybody in this audience who has never tasted alcohol, please raise your hand." Nobody did, not even in the Bible Belt, where you would think some people would never have tasted alcohol. If you don't drink, among your drinking cohorts you are considered an oddball. So probably they did not want to identify themselves. It gave me the opportunity to assume that everybody is still drinking the way I am. Moderately, occasionally, infrequently. Some even heavily, the way Sir Winston Churchill did, but that does not mean that you are an alcoholic. I said, "There are 100 million of us in this country who drink. But there are 10 million of those drinkers who become alcoholics. One out of 10! Let's count off." At the first table, at which 10 were seated, they counted off loud and clear. One, two, three, they stopped at the first 10. I said, "One of you, statistically, is an alcoholic. Which one is it?" Well, there was giggling and one man pointed to his neighbor. I said, "Wait a minute, denial is one of the first signs of alcoholism," and that frightened him. It gave me a wonderful opportunity to talk about some deep-seated attitudes. If they had invited me to speak about cancer, another serious disease, had I said, "Let's assume that statistically, one out of the first 10 of you is already suffering from cancer; who is it?" Nobody would have laughed. Each one would have done some introspection. Am I losing weight? Do I have a lump somewhere? Am I bleeding from an orifice? Each one would have gone through the symptoms and early signs to see if he or she were that 1 out of 10. The rest of the audience would never have giggled, never have pointed a finger. Instead they would have reached out with deep concern and compassion if anybody had been identified as a cancer victim. Not so with alcoholism. Because deep down we have yet to plumb the attitude that alcoholism is not really a disease. Even many people who say it is, I think, really give it lip service. When push comes to shove as it did when I was almost failing with that patient, I had a tendency to deny the disease nature of alcoholism.

Another difficulty in terms of attitudes was clearly shown in an industrial arbitration hearing. I want to read from the *NCA Labor-Management Alcoholism Journal*, a very useful and fascinating publication that gives news of what is happening all over the country in this field. There was a landmark decision in Pennsylvania last year made in favor of a plaintiff who complained that he had been fired unjustly by Crucible, Inc., a Pittsburgh firm. It went up to arbitration. The company had an alcoholism policy and this man, who was apparently a top executive and who had gone around lecturing on the policy to other management individuals, was well aware of it. He was directed into the treatment program. He went to a doctor and let me read from the doctor's letter in the hearing: "As you know, I examined (Mr. X) on February 9, 1971. The positive findings then were palpable liver-edge two finger breadths below the right costal margin. Some depression of mental function. Tremors of arms, dry coarse skin, inflamed pharnyx and coated tongue." Then there was a series of abnormal laboratory findings I won't burden you with. The doctor continued with,

> He was encouraged to seek help in quitting drinking at the clinic for alcoholics. He agreed to do this. But after one visit there he decided he preferred to see a private psychiatrist. He stated that after seeing the derelicts at this clinic he realized he didn't want to get into that condition. When I saw him on February 16, just a week later, he had had no alcoholic drinks for one week, except for one or two beers a day. He looked like a different person. He had increased mental alertness and minimal tremors of the hands. His tremors were controlled with Valium. He did not develop DT's. He had been eating three good meals a day and his nutritional state was much improved. He was scheduled to see a private psychiatrist the next week of February 23, and I will follow him periodically for evaluation of his liver condition.

Well, the long story is that this man was not helped by continuing to drink. Psychiatrists, apparently also, regard one or two beers as nothing reprehensible and he went down and down. His job performance was poor and so the company fired him. He finally got to Gateway, a rehabilitation recovery center in Pittsburgh where Dr. Twersky, a fellow psychiatrist, was treating him. Now Dr. Twersky recognizes the nature of alcoholism and made sure the man stopped drinking completely. Different, apparently, from the other physicians who regarded alcoholism as a Valium deficiency, he realized it was an entity in itself. When the man was helped with Antabuse, with AA, and with supportive services from Al-Anon, he recovered and sued the company. The verdict in arbitration was that the company was guilty. They paid him all his back pay.

I have learned that my early attempts to analyze deep-seated psychological conflicts was a mistake before the man quits drinking completely. It is impossible to determine what is really primary, whether it is alcoholism or some deep-seated psychiatric disease process, such as schizophrenia or depressive psychosis, unless you begin first or simultaneously to treat alcoholism as an entity in itself. My gut reaction is that more than 90 percent of my patients (when my secretary totaled up recently, I was amazed that I had seen 5,000 alcoholics) were primary alcoholics. All the psychological symptoms and the psychiatric diagnoses that these people were so prone to in the state mental hospitals, were a *result* of the alcoholism and not the cause. Because as soon as the alcoholism was treated appropriately and they recovered, all these neuroses and seeming psychoses, disappeared. I can truthfully say that the great bulk of my alcoholic patients are no more neurotic than you or I. That may not be saying much, I'll grant you that.

This brings up an attitude that I think is so inimical and so much a threat to our programs across the country that I wish to say something about it. Namely, that nobody twists the alcoholic's arm to take a drink. After all, he takes a drink where there is a certain amount of free will involved. That is what we rely on to get him to stay sober. Can't you say that because of this phenomenon, the alcoholic is responsible for being an alcoholic? After I get through pouring out my heart and all of you get through doing your darndest to help the alcoholic client or patient, he sometimes leaves your office as mine sometimes did and goes to the corner bar and has a drink. Can't you say that the alcoholic is responsible for being an alcoholic?

How many of you would raise your hands with me and say that one can make this statement and should, as matter of fact, hold the alcoholic responsible for being an alcoholic. Let's see a show of hands. Yes, I see a sprinkling of hands and if I lowered my voice a little more and became a little more seductive and used more entrapment, I could probably entice more of you into making this statement. I have just trapped a number of you, and yet, in my heart, I can't really blame you for a judgment about an alcoholic that you would never make if your patient were a diabetic.

Nobody holds the diabetic responsible for being a diabetic. We don't know the causes of diabetes really. In some few cases we do, but why the pancreas goes haywire, we really don't know. The involvement of the hypothalamus has also been established by experiments in dogs, but we just don't fully understand. The diabetic becomes a diabetic through no fault of his or her own. We know about the hereditary involvement and we know that eating sugar does not cause diabetes. There are people who eat a lot more sugar than do many people who develop diabetes. How many of you in the audience are diabetic? Anybody? Yes. A few of you. How many of you know of a diabetic patient in your family or that you work with? Many more. I am sure you have never felt in the cockles of your heart that the diabetic must be held responsible for being a diabetic. I have been in emergency rooms when a diabetic has gone off his diet and comes into the emergency room sometimes in a second or a third diabetic coma, and I have never heard a nurse or a doctor look at the diabetic and say, "You dirty diabetic." But with the alcoholic that used to be par for the course.

We don't know the causes of alcoholism either. Drinking alcohol alone is not the cause of alcoholism, otherwise we would almost all be developing alcoholism. There are many, many factors involved that we haven't yet teased apart. So we should not hold the alcoholic responsible for being an alcoholic because it is not his fault. However, I trapped some of you excellent people in the audience into making that statement because I did not clear up a confusion that I glossed over. You never hold the diabetic responsible for being a diabetic, but you should hold the diabetic responsible for *treating* it. The same is true with alcoholism. We must learn how to hold the alcoholic responsible for *treating* his alcoholism. It is his responsiblity, but not his alone. And the same is true for diabetes. Society has discovered all sorts of diet drinks to help the diabetic but society doesn't really help the alcoholic stay sober. Instead, let an alocholic be invited to a cocktail party and if he goes, as fortunately he might and still not drink, he very often finds that his host is a pusher. "Ah, come on, have one, it can't hurt you. You could be the life of the party!" I used to do that myself. Oh no, the alcoholic gets very little help in society in terms of support and in terms of social attitudes.

I would like now to turn to the promise. That involves another threat, a threat that we have discovered is so useful in turning the picture around 180 degrees. Lest you think that I am bitter, lest you think I am discouraged, let me tell you that I am always on cloud nine when I think about the alcoholism field. I feel enormously enthusiastic about the promise that lies ahead of us because we have discovered a threat which is tremendously important. It was first discovered, meaningfully, in 1935, when that remarkable fellowship of AA was founded in Akron, Ohio, by these two drunks who got together, Bill Wilson and Bob Smith, and discovered they could help each other stay sober by sharing their fears and problems and hopes. They shared it with others and it was remarkably successful. One of the dicta of AA (and there are other marvelously juicy aphorisms that are so appropriate to one's work) is that a person gets to be so sick of being sick that he or she no longer wants to be sick. That starts him or her on the upturn of recovery.

We have extended that. The threat of job loss has been one of the most dramatic turning points in the experiences of hundreds and thousands of alcoholics across the country. As a matter of fact, one of our District Court judges in Maryland, is himself a recovered alcoholic and makes no bones about it while he is on the bench. Whenever he gets a DWI, often even the first time, the judge sets a sentence of 90 days in jail with the alternative of going to 90 AA meetings for the next 90 days. His recovery rate is phenomenal. He has such a low recidivism rate that he is the envy of all the other judges. They perhaps do not quite have the conviction needed to take this step that he has taken. When an industry does have the courage and the forethought to develop an alcoholism program based on the threat of job loss for diminished or poor job performance the turnabout is dramatic. We have seen across the country some remarkable statistics from the early pioneers—Eastman Kodak, Allis Chalmers, DuPont, Equitable Life Assurance, and many others.

When the Navy adopted its alcoholism program and after a few years awarded a contract to evaluate its programs, the major findings and conclusions of the study were: alcohol abuse results in annual economic losses ranging between $360 million and $680 million per year. Now that is only in the Navy. In the overall we have gone up from a $25 billion industry hangover to a $45 billion one. I can't even keep track of these astronomical figures, they just don't penetrate. But the Navy accurately computed that it was millions and millions of dollars lost due to their alcoholism. The alternative of arbitrarily discharging diagnosed alcoholics and replacing them with new personnel is two times more costly than the present alcoholism rehabilitation initiative program. Most important the advantage in rehabilitating the career personnel group, ages 26 and up, is more than five to one. They recoup their expenses more than five times. Lest you think this information from the Navy does not apply to you or any other industrial program that does not have the same control over its captive population that the military has, here is information from a confidential report by one of the railroads. This railroad now has a six-to-one recovery of their costs after putting in their industrial alcoholic programs. They computed it down to the last penny.

The American Medical Association also finally has seen the light of day. In addition to declaring alcoholism a disease, the AMA began to recognize that their own membership might be diseased. After the pioneering work of Dr. LeClair Bissel who published one of the first studies of alcoholic doctors in *The American Journal of Psychiatry* in October 1976, the AMA has held three national conferences. Now in approximately 30 or more states, there are alcoholism programs usually run by the State Medical Society for alcoholic doctors. These programs are based on the principles that were enunciated way back in 1960 when The National Council on Alcoholism established its labor management consultative service.

All I can tell you is that as we push the early detection of alcoholism further and further back to its earliest development, we are opening the floodgates of preventing alcoholism. The research that Dr. Charles Lieber at Mt. Sinai and those at the Veterans Administration are doing—discovering enzymatic differences in alcoholics before they become alcoholics—is another floodgate opener. The research has not been done on humans yet for obvious reasons. You can't take those liver biopsies as easily in humans as you can in a baboon. Charlie Lieber has developed a baboon colony that is the first animal model of alcoholism close to the evolution of mankind. He has made baboons into alcoholics. (It usually works the other way around.) But some amazing things are only just now coming out.

Research into the genetic aspects of alcoholism also represents some exciting advances. Years ago, when I lectured and someone in the audience asked if alcoholism is inherited, I said, "That's nonsense! There is no evidence that alcoholism is inherited. It is true it runs in families and your risk is higher, but it is not genetic. Why, many things run in families including bank presidencies! The chances of a son of a bank president becoming a bank president are much better than when his father isn't one. But nobody has shown that there is a gene for bank presidencies, forget about it!"

I can't lecture that way now since the work of Goodwin and Schuckit and people in the Scandinavian countries. It is only within the last few years that we definitely know there are biologic and physiologic precursors to alcoholism. It is a disease in every sense of the term. Precisely what the nature is, we still need to be informed and I hope our research budget will increase. But we are mature enough right now to go out, fan out across the country and help many more alcoholics recover and save those wasted lives; save the jobs and the families and the health of these individuals.

When I was a resident in psychiatry, we were told the same about mental illness. I remember vividly a session where the supervisor said to a few of us who were interested in community psychiatry,

> Men, you are much more mature than you think you are. You are not like the little six-year-old whose teenage brother was asked to baby-sit for him when the parents went out that Saturday night. The teenager was angry because he had wanted to see a 'sex' movie that night. Then he suddenly realized he could solve the problem by dragging his kid brother to the movie with him. So there they were watching this torrid scene in the movie, where the hero put his hand under the heroine's blouse. The hero looked her in the eye and said, 'I want what I want when I want it.' The little six-year-old didn't

know what the hero wanted, so he tugged his brother's arm and said, 'What does he want?' The brother said, 'Shut up!' The kid went to bed that night utterly confused. He sneaked into the movie house the next day to watch the same scene, where the hero said, 'I want what I want when I want it.' He still couldn't understand it. The next day at school he couldn't wait until recess. He ran over to his little six-year-old girlfriend in the playground and grabbed her roughly by the shoulder and shook her. You see, he had forgotten some of the details but he remembered to try to lower his squeaky little voice and look her in the eye and say, 'I want what I want when I want it.' The little girl said, 'You'll get what I've got when I get it.'

Now I think we have it in the field of alcoholism and with all of your help we can make a big dent in the problem.

Discussion

Speaker Dr. Maxwell Weisman chaired the panel. Panelists who participated in this discussion were Luther Cloud, M.D., Board Member, National Council on Alcoholism; Herbert Martey, M.A., Director of Alcoholism Programs, South Oaks Hospital; Reverend Peter Sweisgood, O.S.B., Assistant Executive Director of the Long Island Council on Alcoholism; and Richard Zoppa, M.D., Senior Psychiatrist, South Oaks Hospital.

Dr. Zoppa:
I have worked with alcoholics in our program for the last five years. Perhaps that gives me some insight into alcoholism. I have to agree with everything Dr. Weisman said this morning. I thought he was going to talk on the threat of alcoholism, and I was very pleased that he talked about the threat of those professionals who deal with alcoholism. When he made the comparison of the alcoholic with a diabetic who, in fact, is never accused of being a diabetic by any physician or paramedic, I thought that perhaps, it wasn't quite as

appropriate as, let's say, using the schizophrenic who is no more considered responsible for his delusions or his hallucinatory experiences than a diabetic is for his diabetes. The etiology of behavior is unknown in both cases. Although, as Dr. Weisman pointed out, the alcoholic raises his elbow, and takes a drink, there are heredity and environmental influences that cause him to do this; for this reason he is a diseased individual as much as, let's say, the schizophrenic or the manic-depressive. I don't mean to say that he is necessarily an emotionally disturbed individual, but he has as much a disease as the emotionally disturbed person.

In order to work with people who suffer from the disease of alcoholism, you first have to look at yourself and truly understand that the individual is suffering from a disease. Further, my experience has been that, without AA, individual endeavors to work with alcoholism generally fail. I have worked with alcoholics individually, without the help of AA and with AA involvement, and there is a tremendous difference in the outcome. People without the support of AA do not fare that well and professionals have to understand that they are not going to be as effective if they are working as an individual; it is too far-reaching a problem.

Rev. Sweisgood:

I am an alcoholic, and I have been working with the Long Island Council for the last 10 years. We have done many things with industry—Grumman Aerospace, Long Island Lighting, *Newsday*—especially in the realm of education. We find that an industrial program is apt to work or fail on the basis of the enlightenment of the supervisors.

Dr. Cloud:

I have been medical director of a large insurance company for 21 years. We've had a program all these years and I can tell you that it works. It doesn't just work at Equitable; it works in any company that you put it in if you know what you are doing, and if you really tie up all the loose ends so that the suffering alcoholic has no where to go except for help. The recovery rates—and I grant that that is a term that still needs to be defined and we are attempting to define it—in occupational programs are the highest known in the country. The average hospital or rehabilitation center perhaps can get a 45 or 50 percent recovery rate; a good occupational program can get 80 percent. It isn't because the doctors in industry are any better, because we are the same doctors, but because we have a system that works.

Mr. Martey:

I first heard about crisis intervention through job jeopardy at an alcoholism conference at South Oaks in 1971. I was newly entering the field at that time. I am a recovered alcoholic, and my knowledge and experience had been mainly through AA and the motivation that people require by getting into AA. I was very skeptical about the job jeopardy concept. I recall questioning how that approach could possibly work. The alcoholic might remain sober on the job for a while but sooner or later he would go back to drinking. Since then I have discovered that the job jeopardy concept works. In fact it doesn't really matter how you get the alcoholic to stop drinking and it doesn't matter what *his* plan is to go back to drinking. As long as we can get him sober for a time something can penetrate and bring him into sobriety. The sobriety can be maintained through the leverage of threatened loss of job because of poor job performance or behavioral problems.

Prior to 1970, a very limited success existed in the work place by looking for the alcoholic employee. It was an impossible task and wasn't the right route. The shift in emphasis was aimed at looking for certain kinds of behavior patterns and job performance breakdowns that could be observed by the supervisor. This was tied to a method of documentation, a method of confrontation, a recommendation for help—intervention. Through this process and the use of job jeopardy, the new concept was developed. It went under a different label. It was not alcoholism that was being sought, but the troubled employees. The names given to this approach are Employee's Assistance Programs or Occupational Alcoholism Programs.

The effort has proved to be very successful with a high rate of recovery among those who are put into job jeopardy. If there is any problem with the concept, it is that there is still too much ignorance about alcoholism among people in industry as to the nature of occupational alcoholism programs and what is required to put these programs in place.

All too often what happens is that a company accepts the idea, accepts the approach as viable and valid, yet will not really put the necessary effort into installing a program. Installing a program is much more complex than simply hiring an individual to cover the entire work force. But this is the present state of the art in this field. Occupational alcoholism programming is in its early stages and is developing.

There are criteria and standards being developed through ALMACA, the Association of Labor Management Consultants and Administrators in Alcoholism. ALMACA hopes to publish these standards, to set up a credentialing process for companies by establishing guidelines for the kinds of program that should be put into place—what is required in terms of staff, what kinds of functions the staff should perform, what kind of background they should have. This is all in the works. I have been involved with ALMACA on the Standards Committee. There is a long way to go in this field. It is very challenging. There has been a beginning, as I see it, and we have come a long way over the past nine years since our first conference on employee alcoholism problems.

Dr. Weisman:
Some of you may have seen a very dramatic article by Jack Anderson about the airline industry, in which he said

there was only one major carrier whose president will not allow an industrial alcoholism program in, because if there is any pilot who develops alcoholism, he'll fire him. Now one can almost sympathize with this beknighted attitude because piloting a plane is a very sensitive profession, and the president of this company might very easily come to believe that the public will boycott that company if they are aware of the fact that there are alcoholic pilots flying planes. Jack Anderson pointed out that far from this being true, what that airline has done, without a company policy on alcoholism, is to drive the pilots underground and into the cockpit. Since Jack Anderson identified the airline, I don't fly Northwest Orient any longer.

Audience:

I am a practicing psychiatrist in private practice. A 37-year-old male was referred to me by his family physician because he was beginning to have blackouts and tremors. He felt that his gait was somewhat unsteady, and he was frightened that he might be fired if he had an accident. The man is intelligent, a high school graduate, and a self-made maintenance engineer. The only significant background history that came out was that his father had had a drinking problem but had taken a pledge with his local priest and for the past 10 years had been dry. When the patient got through talking about his problem, I suggested that he come into the hospital at least for detoxification. He decided to come in the very next day. When the meeting was over, he asked me, "Doctor, can I ever become a social drinker?" I said, "If you are leaving this office with the idea that you will become a successful social drinker, don't bother coming back." I would like to hear your comments on this.

Dr. Weisman:

That's a beautiful question to begin with. Does anyone want to leap up and answer?

Dr. Cloud:

Why don't we answer it all together! We'll all have different words I thínk, but...

Dr. Weisman:

No, I think the word in every case will be: no, he can never return to social drinking with impunity. Does anyone on this panel differ?

Rev. Sweisgood:

Absolutely not.

Dr. Zoppa:

He can, but he runs a tremendous risk.

Dr. Cloud:

Four years ago in Washington, D.C., we had, in an auditorium larger than this, 52 people on the stage who were all recovered alcoholics. Because it was alphabetical it started with Buzz Aldrin, the astronaut, and ended with Marie Zolotow who writes thousands of articles. In between were Garry Moor, Senator Harold Hughes, Jim Kemper, several physicians, and so forth. This question was asked by the press and I in turn asked the panel to answer it. And 52 voices said: "NO! Never again." As far as we know the only kind of control mechanism is abstinence. When somebody invents or tells us of something better, I hope we are all flexible enough to go along with it. But certainly today, I would say to any patient, and have said to hundreds, you can never drink again. You don't say it that way, you say one day at a time over a period of time. I would be a fool to allow an alcoholic patient to ever think that he can learn to redrink.

Rev. Sweisgood:

I would like to relay a little of my own experience. About two years ago I had a heart attack. I hooked a 260-pound giant sea bass and, typically alcoholic, I fought the thing for three hours and I got it. I went back to the dock with a victorious smile on my face and had a heart attack. I was put in the hospital and I told the doctor that I am an alcoholic and that I can't take mood-changing chemicals like other people do. I hadn't even had an aspirin in almost 10 years. He said, "If I am going to treat you I have got to give you Valium and morphine." I said, "Doctor, I am against suicide, so go ahead and do what you have to do, but on two conditions: one, that it be administered to me by someone other than myself, on your authority, knowing that I am an alcoholic and would prefer not to have anything, and second, that I be withdrawn from everything by the time I leave this hospital." He said, "O.K., you've got both those things." By the second day I found myself really looking forward to the next shot of morphine, the next Valium. By the third day I'd made telephone calls I don't remember making. I called up here and asked for my check and a number of other things I wish I hadn't done. By the evening of the fourth day I was threatening the nurse her job if she didn't call up the doctor and increase the morphine.

Now I don't know—and I don't think anybody else does—what is entailed in addiction. We know about tolerance, we know about withdrawal but what is in between is a great, big mystery. I am telling you that the whole complex mechansim of addiction had gone into gear. I would not have died of Valium addiction or morphine poisoning; but if I believed I could drink socially, I would have gone out there and gone back to my first love and would not be alive today.

You've heard of the Rand Report? This is the Sweisgood Report.

Mr. Martey:

I think that it is important to keep talking about this as it never gets put to rest; because either the alcololic, who is not willing to accept his illness, keeps wanting to go back to drinking with safety, or because many people, who are ignorant about the process of alcoholism, think that a return to drinking is conceivable, if drinking is moderate. The problem, of course, is that the alcoholic is not a moderate drinker. Never was and never can be. I think the analogy made this morning, by Dr. Weisman, about diabetes is accurate here: Once you've got it, you will be an alcoholic. If a person is diagnosed correctly as an alcoholic and is indeed an alcoholic, he will get into serious trouble when he takes alcohol. The diabetic gets into serious trouble with excessive use of sugar. The only thing the alcoholic can do is to stop if he wants to be safe. Once a person has progressed in the illness where he can no longer tolerate or handle alcohol, there is no safety in the use of alcohol for that person.

Dr. Zoppa:

I was being facetious before when I said they can drink at risk. Actually the question that I often get from alcoholics when I treat them is, "Why can't I drink? I have a friend who drank heavily and has been able to drink in a controlled manner." My response to people when that is brought up is, you can go out and drink and fool yourself for an hour, a day, a week, a month, or longer, but at some point along the way a situation will arise when the drinking is just not going to stop. It will interfere with functioning and with life.

Dr. Weisman:

I'd like to tell you an anecdote about my own personal experience with a patient in group therapy. There was a young man of 37 whom I considered almost as my co-therapist. He was a good AA member, he had been sober for a number of years, and he was doing beautifully. But one day he dropped out. He had been part of a core of people who were faithful in coming week after week and I was concerned. He had been divorced and was now living alone. I asked people in the group to look him up. They said he had dropped out of AA meetings in the community and moved away. I thought, well, that's strange that he didn't notify us because it wasn't like him. He was a responsible young man but I thought he might have started to drink and then gone on a "geographic cure." About a year passed and one Saturday afternoon, I was in a supermarket when I ran into him. He was pushing a cart around and had a beautiful young woman with him. I ran over to him and said, "Larry, how nice to see you. What happened?" He got all embarrassed and introduced me to his fiancée with whom he was living. He told me that his fiancée drank and that he would often join her in a drink. For the last year almost, he was drinking and controlling it. "This is God's honest truth," he said. "Larry," I said, "that's fascinating." (Remember, this was years before the Rand Report.) "AA teaches that what you are doing is impossible. Why don't you come back to the group and tell us about it, as a scientist. Maybe it's your girlfriend's perfume or something that is doing this. I think you owe it to us." He was embarrassed and said, "I know how the others would react to me. They'd make me feel that I am a traitor so I decided just to drop out." I pressured him and finally he said, "Well, I'll come next Saturday." But I sensed that he wouldn't and sure enough he didn't show up. I was going to tell the people in the group therapy about this experience, but I forgot. A crisis in the group had come up and I just didn't tell them.

About a month later a young woman came in who was still drinking; it was her first visit and she asked for help. Of course they all pitched in and some of the AA members said, "You have to learn to go without alcohol for the rest of your life but you can do it a day at a time." Then I remembered Larry and said, "Now wait a minute," and I told them that he had been able for almost a full year to drink with control. Well, there was a loud guffaw in the audience. The news had not caught up with me yet. Larry, that week, had been admitted to a state mental hospital in a terrible state.

So I really realized how easy it is to fall into the trap. Sure , almost all of our patients test us. When we tell them to go to AA and that AA's philosophy is that they must be abstinent, there is a need to test authority and to check out things. They almost all do that, at least my patients do, for a longer or shorter period, but everyone in my experience that I know of, has come a cropper.

Audience:

What is being done in industrial programming to address women's problems? We know that identification of women employees is difficult. They are not going to stop with the boys at the local bar after work. They will make sure that their liquor supply is home when they get there. So, they are much more difficult to detect.

Dr. Weisman:

As you can see, I am wearing a button that says, "Alcoholism is a woman's issue." It was issued by the National Council on Alcoholism. It has been one of the most educational things I have done in my long life of trying to educate people. When I walk along the street many women do a double take and ask me, "What does that mean?" I get picked up by more women today than I ever did when I was younger. In an elevator recently, a woman, lowering her voice, asked me that question. I replied, "What do you think it means?" Everybody turned around and looked and by the time we got up to the twenty-fourth floor everybody was talking about alcoholism. Women also become alcoholics but whether or not they do, it is their issue as well. It is one of the most neglected issues in our society.

Dr. Cloud:

First, we have to talk about our terms. For instance, a program in industry is a number of things. First of all, it is an identification program; then it is a treatment program; then it is a follow-up program. Now, as far as I know, the treatment of a woman, of a man, of a black, an Oriental, or an Indian is the same. The treatment is to stop drinking. The treatment is to use AA. I really don't think you use one type of treatment for a man and another type of treatment for a woman. They are both human organisms who have somehow become addicted to alcohol.

But identification is a different story. Actually, what we are trying to do in our program is to seduce or induce people to come for help. If we can seduce them nicely and give them something like good health, good fellowship, and so forth, fine. But if we put a gun to their heads and say, go to the medical department, or the judge says, go to AA or jail for 90 days, we get them into treatment. The important thing is to get them into treatment. I don't think that treatment varies, but I do think the way you get people into treatment may vary, because identification in the work place depends on function. It doesn't depend on whether a person drinks in the club car going home or drinks at the bar or drinks at home. It depends on how they function the next morning. I have seen just as many women in industry hide half pints of brandy or pints of liquor in their closet as I have seen men put them in the desk drawer. It is the same thing. I have seen just as many women come back from a nine-martini lunch as I have seen men. You get them into treatment through the same function. We do not pay people in industry to drink. We pay them to do a job. I think the identification in the work place is the same. But I think you might modify your program somehow to make it easier for the woman to come forward or to make it easier for the boss to lower the boom on the woman. That is where the problem is. It is the old double standard. A tough boss will be able to say to a man, if you keep it up I'll send you to the medical department. But with a woman he takes a different point of view. He says, why don't you try to cut down on your drinking?

I agree with the button, but I am not convinced that we must set up huge programs for women that are different from programs for men, or huge programs for blacks, or huge programs for Orientals.

Mr. Martey:
I agree.

Dr. Weisman:
There is an important difference, perhaps philosophical, that I would like to lay before you. Nobody—black, white, green, or purple—is exactly like everybody else and certainly there are vast differences between men and women. The more individualized the treatment program is the more successful it is. You know that women have different psychological reactions and attitudes. You know that the stigma of being a woman alcoholic is much greater than that of being a male alcoholic. Therefore, that should alter your approach even to get that woman into treatment. And even once she is in AA or in group therapy, there ought to be some ability to recognize what is agitating her, what is going on in that woman's mind and heart, so that you can reach the person with more effective treatment. Now, I feel hot about this because what I have said about women applies also to minorities. It has been one of the shortcomings, I think, in my state that that has not been paid enough attention to. There has got to be a special focus on getting the person *into* treatment but while he or she is in, to recognize these attitudinal and social differences that make it difficult to keep this person in treatment effectively.

Dr. Cloud:
Don't let anything Max and I say confuse you completely because we are saying the same thing; although I am calling it pretreatment, and Max is calling the whole thing treatment. A very dangerous thing in industry is that sometimes, depending on how you are set up, you are not supposed to do treatment. You are supposed to refer. But, as

far as I am concerned, and here I agree with Max, treatment begins when the patient comes in the door and sits down at the desk. That is treatment. But by separating it, I am able to live a little better with my philosophical concepts, which say, you have to make it easier for a woman to destigmatize herself and come forward.

Audience:

Are you encouraging the need for AA to segregate their programs?

Dr. Weisman:

On the contrary. It is much more valuable for all of us to recognize we are all members of the human race. Sometimes, however, it is *essential* to have a specialized group. And we find that often a specialized group is the stepping stone to the more generalized group. We have pilots in AA who call themselves "Birds of a Feather." We have international doctors in AA, "The Caduceus Club." On the Eastern Shore of Maryland, when the blacks felt that they were not welcome in the white AA, they formed their own specialized group, and I felt it was right for the time.

Audience:

How would you classify the weekend alcohol abuser or the problem drinker who is not an alcoholic but who may wind up in a DWI situation, because he drank one too many? How do you classify a person as being an alcoholic?

Rev. Sweisgood:

Loss of control. The difference between the problem drinker and the alcoholic is that the problem drinker still has control. He can accurately and consistently predict, most of the time, how many drinks he is going to have once he begins drinking. At some point in the alcoholic progression he loses the ability to do that. He no longer can accurately and consistently predict how many drinks he is going to have after he begins drinking. Once that loss of control takes place, he is now an alcoholic. You are not a little bit pregnant or not a little bit alcoholic.

With that particular symptom, it is very difficult to ascertain when it happens, how long it takes to happen. It is different with different people. But once that has occurred the individual is now alcoholic.

Say you have two people in a jeopardy situation, and one is a heavy drinker and the other is an alcoholic and they are both having job performance problems. The supervisor says much the same thing to both of them: Your performance has gone down below a certain level and either you do something about it or we are going to have to fire you. Well, the nonalcoholic knows his drinking is getting in the way and he cuts back. Then he doesn't have any more performance problems due to his drinking because he still has control. The alcoholic *thinks* he has control and he tries to control it, but his job performance problems will surface again in the future because he has lost control, and that's a permanent condition.

Audience:

In industry we get the binge drinker who can control his two cocktails a night until there is a big meeting ahead with the boss. Then he goes on a binge, he does not show up, everything collapses. Is he an alcoholic? How can we help him?

Rev. Sweisgood:

Jellinek talks about Alpha, Beta, Gamma, Delta, and Epsilon types of alcoholics. The Alpha is what I think you are talking about. He is the guy who is psychologically dependent, but not physically dependent; when under stress he learned to cope with that stress by means of alcohol. He is not the kind we call diseased; the only diseased kind is the Gamma who is both physically and psychologically dependent on alcohol and who does lose control. The type you are talking about can be thought of as alcoholic and should be treated in much the same way.

Then there is the Beta, who isn't physically or psychologically addicted, but who will develop a disease which, if he continues to drink will kill him; so he has to stop or die. But he is not either physically of psychologically dependent on alcohol.

The Delta alcoholic is the French alcoholic. He drinks all the time, but he never does the things that are characteristic of the Gamma alcoholic because he does not lose his family, he does not wreck the car, he does not go to jail, and so forth. He will probably die 10 to 12 years before he should of a liver problem. The highest cirrhosis count in the world is in France presently.

The Epsilon is the periodic alcoholic who drinks only once a year but when he does, "Katie, bar the door." The trouble with the Epsilon is that the drinking episodes are going to get closer together and he will go over into Gamma alcoholism in time. It is sometimes more damaging than is the Gamma. If your daddy is going to be passed out on the front lawn every morning, you get kind of used to that. But if he straightens up and flies right and gets your respect back, and then the bottom falls out, it is seen as being more damaging.

The kind you are talking about is Alpha and he should be treated as a person who should not use booze. Period.

Audience:

I have a two-part question: First, do we have diagnostic tools available today in the medical profession for determining the existence of alcoholism simply on a biochemical basis? Second, if a doctor indicates to his patient that he is drinking too much, what is the responsibility of the doctor to prescribe treatment?

Dr. Cloud:

The trouble with medicine is that it is not an exact science. The trouble with testing is that it often tells you more of what is *not* the case than what is. In other words there are a number of tests, very definitive, very specific, that will tell you about liver damage but liver damage can come from other hepatic toxins. Liver damage does not diagnose alcoholism although it makes you suspicious. I don't know of any biochemical test that will diagnose alcoholism and I doubt that there ever will be any that will diagnose alcoholism per se.

The best diagnostic tool we have is a suspicious doctor. I think that that is the answer. All the tests do is tell us to look for things and to look further. But, in the long run, the diagnosis of alcoholism is made not by sitting down with the patient one time, but over a period of time, to see what this person does, by looking at function and at loss of control.

There aren't any blood tests to tell you about loss of control, so you observe your patient. The executive who got drunk the time he was supposed to be at a very important meeting is showing you the best loss of control in the world. At the time he should be on his best behavior, he is drunk. What better diagnosis do you have? Quickly we are able to say this man is alcoholic. If I am going to examine a vice-president in my office at two o'clock in the afternoon, and he comes in knowing he is going to be examined, knowing I am going to look down his throat, and he apologizes and says, "If you notice something on my breath, I had four or five drinks with the boys," first of all he is lying and second, he is alcoholic. Because this is the time he knows he should not drink at all. He is denying his own disease.

Audience:

How do you approach a friend you feel is an alcoholic but who is denying the symptoms?

Mr. Martey:

There is no answer. We can only try. This is one of the major problems that we deal with in alcoholism, and one of the major difficulties, of course, is getting through denial.

We call it a symptom of the illness. A person denies alcoholism and that is almost indicative that the person is an alcoholic. Getting through to the individual is extremely difficult if a person is not ready to listen. That is why occupational alcoholism programs are good. The individual may have to listen if he wants to hold on to the job.

The best thing to do is to be very direct and confront your friend. You take a risk because you may lose a friend. If you are very firm in this, however, your friend may thank you later. Usually what happens is that alcoholics run away from their friends, or friends get rid of them because alcoholics don't want to do anything about their drinking unless some kind of leverage is brought to bear. This is what has worked mostly with alcoholics. Leverage through industry, leverage through family court, the possiblity of marriage breakdown. Things like that.

Giving an alcoholic advice—a doctor is telling the alcoholic that he or she suffers from alcoholism and should go for help—is not always the thing that is going to work, but with enough people saying this, the alcoholic may finally get around to doing something.

Dr. Zoppa:

Many people who drink alcoholically are waiting to hear about their behavior. They pretty much flaunt it in your face. They are letting you know in many ways that they drink and are just waiting for someone to say, in a benign way, that they have to do something about stopping.

Rev. Sweisgood:

I like that. In a case like this, if you are the "significant other," go to Al-Anon. There you will find out that you have been perhaps doing the wrong things—playing the role of patsy, rescuer, mother, persecutor, all of which have been feeding into his alcoholism. Learn it is a disease, learn to detach with love, and begin to learn the various things that will, in effect, induce a bottom by the fact of the "significant other" getting well.

Audience:

Is there a possibility that everybody is a potential alcoholic? If so, what can we do in the way of prevention so that we don't become alcoholic?

Dr. Weisman:

That is a fascinating question. When I lecture and somebody asks me if I am an alcoholic, I say, "I am not an alcoholic, *as yet,*" implying I have the potential for becoming alcoholic.

Dr. Cloud:

I think every one of us in this room is susceptible to every type of cancer you can think of, every type of heart disease, hypertension, etc., and alcoholism. If you don't want to become alcoholic, it is very simple. You are considering the *only* disease that I can tell you how *not* to get, and that's by never drinking alcohol.

Mr. Martey:

Prevention is a key question that has been raised since the beginning of AA and the early days at the Yale Center Studies on alcoholism. The first question was, how do we prevent alcoholism? It is still the first question. It hasn't been answered yet. We don't know how to prevent alcoholism, except as Dr. Weisman says, don't drink. I don't know that education in itself is the answer. I really don't know what the answers are for prevention. The problem requires a great deal of effort and attention.

Rev. Sweisgood:

I would like to give some of my own experience from having talked to 2,000 supervisors at Grumman Aerospace. I took about a year and a half to do this. I sometimes revisit plants a year after I have done them and I have had the experience of men calling me aside and saying, "Pete, I heard your lecture a year ago, and I haven't had a drink since." I really have a lot of faith in education. Once a person is alcoholic, education is not of very much value, although I've had alcoholics, with proper education, come for help, too. I think it is an indispensable means of preventing alcoholism. There is always going to be alcoholism, but with a licensed beverage industry such as we have, putting out the fact that alcohol is an aphrodisiac, a status symbol, necessary for your macho—outrageous things that are not true—we have to counteract these things. And I don't think fanaticism is the answer. I don't think the Women's Christian Temperance Union had the right answer. I think that the *truth* is the answer. I think that we have to approach the truth as closely as we can and give that to our young people. I have seen them get up and cheer when they have gotten hold of things that are helpful to them.

Dr. Weisman:

I would like to ask Luther if what he says is true, that everybody is a potential alcoholic. How does he work into that system the recent work on genetics, where some people inherit some of the preconditions that make them more prone than other people who apparently don't inherit it? And how does he account for the fact that 60 percent of the Chinese, who have an extremely low rate of alcoholism, have a flushing reaction when they take a drink, almost like an Antabuse reaction, and they are very uncomfortable. Those Chinese do not drink more than a sip or two. How do you account for genetics if you say that everybody can develop alcoholism?

Dr. Cloud:

What I said was, everyone has a *chance*. I was very careful, I didn't say an *equal* chance. I think I have a chance, by going out today and buying a lottery ticket, of winning a million dollars. But I don't think I have a very *good* chance of it. Certainly we are familiar with the work in genetics and we know that some of these reactions have something to do with it. But I think that, even though I am not an Oriental and even though I don't have a genetic background in alcoholism so far as I know, I have a chance, I hope it is very small, of becoming alcoholic. We all have a chance—but not equal.

At the present stage of our knowledge, we would have to say that everybody runs the risk of developing alcoholism, because we don't know the causes of alcoholism. We are investigating a great many factors, some of which may have more weight than others, but we still don't know and, until we do, we'll have to say everybody runs a risk.

Audience:

A friend told me recently, and this has confused me a bit, that he is an alcoholic, but he is one of the fortunate ones because his was a psychological dependency, so now he can drink. But what I have learned here is that there are no levels of differentiation. If you are alcoholic, you are alcoholic. Or am I wrong?

Rev. Sweisgood:

Well, I think that a person who has ever had a problem, psychological, physical, or both runs a tremendous risk in ever picking up a drink. That is what we're all saying. He is playing games. The guy who jumped the curb in Brooklyn and killed six people could have been me. That is why I don't drink. The risk is too great. You might go home 999 times and just go to sleep and not bother anybody, but there is that one time when you wake up in the morning and go out to repark your car and find it splashed with blood. There is too much at stake here.

Dr. Weisman:

We don't have to know the causes of a disease to be able to develop stages in the natural history of that disease. We don't know the cause of the cancer, but we know there are stages one, two, three, and four. It is a mistake to say, just because there is uncertainty about the etiology, that there is uncertainty about the development or even about the treatment.

Audience:

What are the characteristics of alcoholism that make it a disease?

Dr. Weisman:

Again, an important question. Why should it be defined as a disease?

Dr. Cloud:

Years ago, before any of us were around, disease had something to do with the fact that it could be communicated from one person to another, and that there was a salient description that could be utilized for that disease. Pneumonia is something that isn't just a cough, because a cough can be many things. So there must be a single description and there must be a host, and there must be an incipient cause. Where we are hung up in alcoholism, as we have told you time after time, is that we do not know the cause. We do not know the cause or causes of schizophrenia, but I don't think anyone is going to argue that schizophrenia is not a disease.

We have gone to all kinds of depths to try to find some criteria by which we can diagnose alcoholism. The problem with alcoholism is that usually it is diagnosed on an emotional basis. I don't drink very much; he drinks a lot; he must be alcoholic. One of the jokes is, an alcoholic is a man who drinks as much as you do but goes to a different church. The emotional concept. We can't live with that scientifically.

Here is what makes alcoholism a disease as far as I am concerned. One, you have very definite classifications that we talked about but that are stages of the same disease: Alpha, Beta, Epsilon, etc. Second, it cannot be transmitted; it is not contagious from one person to another, so we have to throw out the communicability. It is something to be described as a loss of control, something that is inherent in all alcoholics. The alcoholic is an individual who does not always know how much he is going to drink. He may, on one or two occasions, but he is always in jeopardy that he cannot stop when he says so. When the bar closes at three o'clock and everybody else goes home, he goes to an after-hours place or he has his own booze hidden away. When the cocktail hour is over at six o'clock, he is the guy who ordered three drinks and takes them to the table and then goes back to the bar. He has lost the ability to control. So if there is one salient feature it is that loss of control, measured by dysfunction.

Now aside from that, there are a number of psychological and physiologic things found in the alcoholic that are not found anywhere else. One, is the so-called blackout, which is not a passing out, not a comatose thing. It is a sleep walking, almost like a state of amnesia, in which the alcoholic will do things, do them surprisingly well, and have no remembrance. Now, except for one or two types of brain damage that usually don't last—because with a brain tumor a person dies very quickly—the blackout is symptomatic only of alcoholism. That is what makes it a disease. Let me be literary rather than scientific for a moment and bring you back to the roots of the word, "disease," which are two Greek words. "Dis," meaning away from as in distance, and "ease," a sense of comfort. If any of you have ever seen an active alcoholic you will see someone as far from a sense of comfort as you will ever see.

Audience:

What are the components of an alcoholism treatment program? How do you treat alcoholics?

Mr. Martey:

Depending on the type of treatment, whether it is inpatient, outpatient, etc., we will take it through various steps. If it is inpatient treatment, a person has to be detoxified. That is a basic medical procedure which usually is accomplished with some medication, such as tranquilizers, anticonvulsants, and vitamins. The procedure should be supervised by a physician and watched by nurses, and within a period of four to five days, the patient can usually be brought safely through detoxification. However, that is just the beginning stage of treatment for the alcoholic. From that point on, when the person is in closer touch with reality, there are a number of approaches that are helpful. The primary goal in treatment is to bring the individual to a state where he or she will not go back to drinking. This is both the short-term and the long-term goal. There may be some work on modification of behavior patterns. Education is necessary to teach the individual about his disease. Most people don't understand the nature of this disease. The family should be involved in the treatment process. Individual and group counseling for the patient and the family are a must. We here at South Oaks use a psychiatrically based treatment approach, where the psychiatrists will deal with the emotional, psychological, and psychiatric problems. The counseling staff will deal with other problems relating to alcoholism. We try to involve the patient in AA because we feel that AA, the concept and approach to sobriety in AA, is the best means of holding on to sobriety. It is a continuation and reinforcement of sober living.

By bringing the patient along through therapy, trying to get at some of the difficulties that make his life stressful, that make it difficult for him to contend with reality situations, by trying to overcome those problems, we introduce a person to situations where he can identify and improve his behavior. All this improves the prospects for his future sobriety. We don't know how long that takes. The treatment can be ongoing, inpatient, outpatient, and for a long period of time.

A person might need to go back and rely on a therapist, and have contact with that person along with AA. If we put a person through treatment, keep a person sober, involved in AA, work with him in some sort of continuing recovery program for a period of 12 months, he has a good chance of holding on to his sobriety for some time.

Audience:
What success rate do you have?

Mr. Martey:
Well, I can speak for South Oaks Hospital because we have been making a study of treatment outcome for the past three-and-a-half years and we have been following our discharged patients. Based on the information we have gathered we have close to an 89 percent success rate of patients who have been sober for more than one year. I can't speak for the results in other treatment facilities.

Audience:
Does a person have to hit bottom before he or she can be helped to recovery?

Rev. Sweisgood:
In the early years it was thought that an alcoholic had to hit bottom before he could get well. We still use the term; a lot of people don't like it. If we define bottom as that point in which it becomes more painful to continue drinking than to stop drinking, then the alcoholic would usually hit bottom laying on Skid Row in borrowed clothes with his fly open, 65 years old with a cirrhotic liver, and a wet brain. Then he got that moment of insight, and said, my god, it wasn't my wife, the boss, the job, it was my drinking. He'd crawl over to the Salvation Army and get a bowl of soup and if somebody had the good sense to get him into AA, he would begin to recover. But there was very little left to recover. This is the kind of person that would come into the

program early in its history. Since that time we have discovered that you can actually induce that bottoming-out process if you are a judge, if you are an employer, if you are a wife, a daughter. It can be done in many different ways. There is no one way to do it. Industry has the very best tools, because by the time a guy gets that far his job usually means more to him than God, country, wife, boss, and everything else. It is the source of the money with which he buys the booze. It is also the source of whatever shreds of self-respect are between him and putting a gun in his mouth and blowing the back of his head off. That is why they have such a tremendous success rate in using the job—"either do something about your performance or you haven't got the job." But in any case, no alcoholic ever quits drinking because he just decided it was the pious thing to do. There is always coercion—either a fatty liver, or an employer, a wife, or a husband who just won't put up with it any more.

Audience:

We worked for years to get an alcoholism program started in our company and now we find that the program is being cut way back. What the hell can we do?

Dr. Weisman:

If everyone were as knowledgeable and as sophisticated as the people in this room, there would be no problems. But the problem is that everyone isn't. All I can say is keep trying and keep trying. You have to believe in it yourself.

Dr. Cloud:

We can prove as we mentioned today, that these programs will save five and six times their cost. We can prove it. Why is it you can go into huge companies and little companies and prove it, and you don't get your program. I don't know, and I have been doing it for 21 years. I still have people say to me, it won't work, we don't need it, we don't have alcoholics here. The president of a very large drug company said, we don't have any alcoholics in our company. I said, "I wish I knew what you put in your air conditioners, we would like to put it in ours." I don't know why but you have to keep trying. I'll tell you one thing I suspect. I suspect that somewhere up in the hierarchy there is an individual who either has a problem or thinks he has a problem, or is afraid he has a problem, and he doesn't want to find out about his problem.

Audience:

Is Antabuse still being used and how effective is it?

Dr. Zoppa:

Yes, Antabuse is being used. My own personal experience is that you can get as many people to stay away from alcohol permanently without Antabuse as you can with it. I don't believe that Antabuse, which can be unpleasant at times and have extremely dangerous effects, is necessary if you have good AA backup. I agree with Herb Martey that alcoholism is a multifaceted entity.

What it gets down to is that the individual who drinks alcoholically will have to learn how to deal with himself, with his feelings, and how he or she is going to get along with the rest of society. In order to do that, I think it takes a lot more than Antabuse. Antabuse as a treatment is a simplification of a very complex problem.

Rev. Sweisgood:

I think that Antabuse has uses, but as long as a person is taking Antabuse solely without AA, he is not motivated to lengthen his fuse, to relate with other people, to get permanently the things that he needs to be more comfortable without the booze than he was with it. He is not motivated. He is motivated by fear of headaches and nausea and vomiting and all the ugly things that go with drinking on top of Antabuse. However, there are certain instances when it is useful. I know a doctor, for instance, who is alcoholic and when she goes to conventions where she used to imbibe a good deal and there is no AA meeting around she will, for insurance, take Antabuse during that period and stop it right after the convention. That is an instance where Antabuse is used successfully. Antabuse is also helpful for people who can't get into a rehab or detox program, who need time behind them to get enough perspective to see what they were doing to themselves. I think it has its uses but with limitations.

Dr. Weisman:

One of my medical colleagues, a recovered alcoholic woman physician, would use Antabuse when she was in a situation where she recognized the same factors that used to get her to drink and kept her drinking—when she was in a strange city, when she was holed up in a hotel where there were stresses, strangers, etc. So she just fortifies herself with Antabuse to get over that stressful period. I find Antabuse a very useful adjunct but never alone because it can be very confusing to the patient to feel that the only treatment for alcoholism is a pill. So I use it, when I do, always in conjunction with a person going to AA. Nobody that I know of in Maryland accuses an AA member who is on Antabuse of using a crutch. It can be very useful to use a crutch when you have a broken leg.

When I went to my first AA meeting as a nonalcoholic, interested in hearing what was said to help other alcoholics, I began to realize that AA is a fellowship that focuses on a change in the life style of victims of this dread disease of alcoholism. I thought how wonderful it is, because that is the answer to the problem of alcoholism for my patients. Then I became kind of addicted to AA meetings. I must confess that I enjoy them enormously and I go to as many open AA meetings as I can when I have some free time. I come away with the conviction that that life style—the things that AA members learned about themselves from the genius of the two cofounders and from all the other members—is useful for non-alcoholics. I have done a good deal of introspection and I came to the conclusion that I learned more from attending AA meetings and looking into myself than I learned from years of analytic-oriented treatment. I would like to recommend to anyone in this audience who is not an alcoholic and who has never been to an AA meeting, to please do yourself a favor and go to a number of AA meetings, because no two of them are alike. You can't judge from one what the other will be like or what you will get out of another AA meeting. Go to several. I guarantee you that if you listen with open ears and an open heart it will be a wonderful experience for all of you. I want to thank all of you for having made this conference one of the most exciting that I have ever participated in.

Chapter 2

DRUG ABUSE PREVENTION COMES OF AGE IN THE 1980s

Robert L. DuPont, M.D.*

It is always exciting to follow Max Weisman. He does those speeches with such authority and is so casual about it that I often think he must use the same speech over and over again. But as many times as I have heard him, he has a new

---

*Dr. DuPont was the Director of the National Institute on Drug Abuse from its creation in 1973 until 1978. He is currently president of the nonprofit Institute for Behavior and Health, Inc., in Washington, D.C., and, as a part of his practice of psychiatry he directs Washington's first phobia treatment program. Dr. DuPont, who received his M.D. degree from Harvard Medical School in 1963, is a Diplomate of the American Board of Psychiatry and Neurology, and a Fellow of the American Psychiatric Association. He is Chairman of the Drug Dependence Section of the World Psychiatric Association, a position he has held since 1974. In 1978, he was awarded the highest honor in U.S. Public Health Service, the Superior Service Award, by the Surgeon General.

Dr. Dupont has written more than 100 professional articles and one book on a variety of topics in the fields of health promotion, drug abuse prevention, and criminal justice. He holds the faculty positions of Associate Clinical Professor of Psychiatry and Behavioral Sciences at the George Washington University School of Medicine and Visiting Associate Clinical Professor of Psychiatry at Harvard Medical School.

story every time. He brings a sense of excitement and commitment to the field that is infectious.

Max had some great stories about clinical encounters. I would like to share an encounter I had this morning with a cab driver. It lacks, perhaps, some of the great sweep of Max's comments, but it has immediacy in the local setting. I told the cab driver that I was going to talk about drug and alcohol problems. As the long ride from the airport went on, he told me about his life. He had been in the service in the Korean War. When he came back from the war he became addicted to heroin, spending a year and a half addicted to intravenous heroin use in the mid-1950s, and then he stopped. I asked him how he'd quit. That was in an era when there wasn't much treatment. He described a situation in which his family, it was a very close family, would not let him in the house as long as he stayed addicted to heroin. He described in particular a very moving experience when he was hungry and needed some food. His mother would feed him only if he would stay outside the house. One rainy day she passed him the food, the chicken, the gravy, and the mashed potatoes. He described the water dripping off the eaves so that the more he ate the gravy, the more there was, and the more diluted it became. He knew then that wasn't any kind of life for him. He stopped his heroin use because he felt the pride of his family. He wanted to rejoin his family more than he wanted the next fix. A few years later he had some problems in his marriage. This led to the onset of a period of alcoholism that lasted much longer and had a much more serious impact on his life than did the heroin problem. He has licked that problem, too. He no longer drinks at all. He stopped drinking because a physician who had treated him for a gallbladder problem advised him, simply, that drinking was bad for his health. As often happens, the threat of serious illness was a real turning point. As Max said, physicians who will take a broader interest in their patients can often contribute in dramatic ways to their health.

To continue the saga of the importance of drugs and alcohol in this man's life, he now has a 27-year-old son who is an alcoholic. The major concern he has in his life now is to help his son stop drinking. The son has not yet made the decision to stop. That one life illustrates the complex and serious impact of the problem of substance abuse in our society. As Max said earlier today, in any of our personal lives, and in our families, we don't have to go far to find the serious negative impact of drugs and alcohol.

One might ask, what is the nature of this problem, is it a disease? And if it is, as most of us now believe, is it one disease ("substance abuse") or is it as many separate diseases as there are drugs? Did the cab driver have two diseases (heroin addiction and alcoholism) or one disease?

I tend to think about these problems as separate but related: they can be thought of in psychological or physiologic terms as *dependence on reinforcing substances*. We have a number of chemicals, a relatively small number actually, that produce feelings that people like, feelings of pleasure that are regularly associated with the intake of substances. These are often called psychoactive substances or *primary reinforcing substances*. Max was talking about the baboons and booze. There is a problem with animal models of dependence on most of these reinforcing substances because the animals often have to be taught to take the substance, whether it's heroin or alcohol or marijuana. Once they learn to take it, they usually become dependent on it. The drug becomes an important part of their lives.

In the drug abuse research field, the great breakthrough has been the self-administration of drugs intravenously to laboratory animals, so that researchers are able to short-circuit the process of taste that often keeps animals from becoming dependent on a particular drug. With intravenous self-administration, the animals get the immediate effect on the central nervous system of the substance. All of the substances that we associate with substance abuse disorders produce the phenomena of reinforcement in *all* laboratory animals. Not just young animals or old animals, or white animals, or black animals, or rich animals, or poor animals. It is a basic biologic reaction of a primary reinforcing substance.

Let me just mention an advertisement that helps make my point. Frank Perdue gets on the air and says that his chickens are terrific because they eat better than we, the listeners. He urges us to eat his chickens because they eat what he tells them to eat, what is good for them. We, by contrast, eat what we like. That choice we have creates tremendous disorders in our diet, as individuals and as a nation. This one ad captures very nicely one of the most fundamental problems in our field: the problem of choice, the problem of each individual determining how he or she will live, and what substances he will take. Many of us would like to help people, like Frank Perdue's chickens, to eat better and stop using (or at least "abusing") drugs. The ultimate problem we have to deal with is the choice that each person makes each day of his life.

We are familiar with the long history of people's exposure to reinforcing substances, alcohol having a particularly long and complex history. In the drug field, our focus is often much more on the immediate past. I am going to give you a few figures about the dimensions of drug abuse in the United States today that might surprise you. I am going to focus particularly on marijuana, but not by any means limit myself to that drug.

You may be surprised to know that out of roughly 170 million Americans over the age of 12, we have 43 million who have used marijuana at least once and 16 million who used it during the last month. Heroin—there are about two million who have used that drug, and about half a million who have used it during the last month. Cocaine—10 million have used it in the United States, two million in the last month.

Now let's talk about the medical use of reinforcing substances or psychoactive drugs. For purposes of this presentation I will break this broad area into three classes:

stimulants, sedatives, and tranquilizers. You may be surprised to know that at some time in their lives, 20 million Americans have taken prescription stimulants, 34 million have taken sleeping pills, and 60 million have taken tranquilizers. Within the last month, two million Americans have taken a stimulant drug like an amphetamine, seven million have taken a sleeping pill, and 17 million have taken a tranquilizer.

Nonmedical use of these prescription drugs is also substantial and, in some cases, almost as large as the medical use. Thirteen million Americans have used stimulants during their lifetimes—nine million have used sedatives and 13 million have used tranquilizers—outside of medical supervision. The use within the last month—1.7 million have taken stimulants, 1.0 million have taken sedatives, and 1.3 million have taken tranquilizers.

Now I want to focus on marijuana because these figures are alarming. Of the over-age-35 population in the United States—from the marijuana point of view, that is "over the hill"—only 1 percent of Americans have used marijuana in the last month, and only 7 percent of the people in this country over the age of 35 have ever used marijuana even once. If we look at the group aged 12 to 17 in the country, we find that 28 percent have used marijuana, and 16 percent of this young population have used marijuana during the last month. If we go to the 18- to 21-year-olds, the rate of use leaps to 59 percent who have used the drug with 31 percent use of marijuana in the last month. In the group aged 22 to 25, marijuana use peaks at 62 percent who have ever used the drug, and the current use has fallen off slightly to 24 percent. Then there is a dramatic drop in the 26 to 34 age group; in the past month only 12 percent, half what it was just a few years earlier, are current users. The ever used rate drops to 44 percent for this age group. So those of us who are over 35 and are thinking about the marijuana use rates need to know about the age relationships, which are different for marijuana than they are for alcohol.

More startling perhaps, are the daily use figures for marijuana. For example, last year among American high school seniors, 29 percent used tobacco every day. I suppose you are not surprised by that figure. You may not know that 6.1 percent of American high school seniors used alcohol every day in their senior year. The marijuana daily use figure among American high school seniors last year was 11 percent. One out of nine American high school seniors now uses marijuana every day in his senior year! One out of nine. You may be surprised to know that these figures are not strongly related to social class. The upper classes use about as much marijuana as the lower classes do. The alcohol and tobacco rates for daily use of high school seniors have been about level during the last few years. The marijuana number has doubled from 6 percent to 11 percent in the last three years. This explosive growth shows no sign of abating. There is no break in that rising trend in the daily use of marijuana.

I am almost ready to stop giving you numbers. When did this marijuana use among today's youth begin? Among Americans who are 12- to 13-years-old (now these are sixth and seventh graders), 8 percent have used marijuana in their lifetimes and 4 percent have used marijuana during the last month; that is, they are "current users." Four out of every one hundred 12- to 13-year-olds have used marijuana in the last month in the United States. Among 14- to 15-year-olds, the lifetime use is 29 percent and the last month figure is 15 percent. Among 16- to 17-year-olds it is 47 percent and 29 percent, and among 18-year-olds it is 60 percent and 40 percent.

Those numbers are, I suspect, staggering to you; they are staggering to me. We have had some rather substantial misfiring in our marijuana prevention efforts during the last decade. We have generally overlooked the dramatic growth of marijuana use. Let me mention that most of this marijuana epidemic has taken place within the last decade. The percentage of Americans who had used marijuana in 1964 was only 2 percent of the adult population. For example, among college students in 1967 the rate of ever use was around 4 percent. I am sure you at this conference are aware of the fact that the increase in marijuana use has brought no reduction whatsoever in the levels of alcohol use among youth. Sometimes, it is said, "We would rather have our kids on...." You fill in the blank. Some people would rather have them on alcohol and some people would rather have the kids using marijuana. The point is that these drug-using behaviors are linked. As the alcohol use figure goes up in any group, the marijuana use figure goes up and vice versa. Pot and booze are not two sides of a teeter-totter. They are clearly linked behaviors.

What happened in the last decade? What produced this dramatic rise in marijuana use? This is the most fascinating question in the drug abuse field. We are not talking about recently discovering a problem that was there all the time, although, obviously, there were precursors to this epidemic before the last decade. Something important has happened. It is not like the hula-hoop fad—it will not simply pass if we ignore it. The trends, the levels of use of marijuana will be much more enduring than that. This marijuana epidemic is presenting us with problems that few of us are comfortable with or are prepared to deal with. I can take some guesses at some of the reasons for the epidemic, but I will admit that these are only guesses.

The main event was the triggering of a chain reaction once a critical threshold was reached. The primary reason for that chain reaction can be found in the demography of the country: a tremendous explosion in the relative and absolute numbers of young people occurred during the last decade. This burst of the youth segment of our population was associated with, as we are all painfully aware, a reduction in the restraining forces, or as some old-timers might say, the "civilizing forces" within our society. Many behavioral constraints that were reasonably effective in earlier decades were diminished or nonexistent during the period 1969 to

1979. Of course we are now, as a nation, entering a period where the number of teen-agers in the country is beginning to shrink. One might expect the demography to now help us solve the marijuana problem. I don't think that that will be the case. A trend toward greater levels of marijuana use has been started and it is not going to be changed back by demography alone.

Part of what sustained this explosive increase and chain reaction had to do with economics. Most of you from the alcohol field are familiar with the impact of economics on the levels of alcohol consumption in this society. There are a lot of people who have a major economic stake in drinking behavior. They are certainly out promoting their self-interests by encouraging people to drink more. The same is true for drug use, although we do not see marijuana billboards, yet.

Let me now sketch some of the long-term trends, about where we might be going. I am sure by now you think I am peddling doom and gloom. Not so. Those of you in the alcoholism field can help give some perspective to the drug abuse field. If you look at alcohol consumption rates in the United States since the end of Prohibition, of course there has been a sharp, general upward trend. The per capita consumption of alcohol has shown a substantial rise. It has apparently leveled off in the most recent years, but in any event it has risen dramatically over the last 40 years.

On the other hand, if you look at the per capita consumption of alcohol in the United States over the last 150 or 200 years you see a rather different and much more positive picture. The forces that led to the Temperance Movement, at the turn of the century, are very deeply ingrained in our society. They have had an effect on drinking levels in this society. The actual per capita consumption is now about the same or less than it was in the nineteenth century, and the per capita consumption *among drinkers* is very much down. There was a much higher percentage of nondrinkers; also, those who drank at all drank much larger amounts of alcohol in the nineteenth century than is true today. You may also be surprised to know that our national appetite for prescription psychoactive drugs is also abating. We are now seeing fewer Valium prescriptions in the United States. The prescription of tranquilizers peaked in the United States in 1975 and has come down every year since. Last year there was about a 10 percent reduction in prescriptions for psychoactive drugs. Those of you who have stock in the drug companies need not worry: their profits have been sustained. The drug companies simply increased the prices! Sleeping pill prescriptions peaked in 1973 and are showing an even more dramatic decline.

I have a fantasy, a dream, a hope, that 10 or 20 years from now the use of sleeping pills will seem as anachronistic as the use of the enema now does. Thirty or forty years ago, most Americans were desperately concerned about having a daily bowel movement. Today that issue, and the health practices it gave rise to, seem close to the bloodletting of a century earlier. Our current preoccupation with getting eight hours of uninterrupted sleep every night is equally misguided and nearly as universal. If you sleep a few hours less on a particular night or if you wake up early, you don't have to take a pill. More and more Americans are learning to be as accepting and understanding of the variation in sleeping patterns as a normal part of their psysiology as most of us now feel about the fact that we may not have a bowel movement on a particular day.

As a society, we are heading toward a much more conservative attitude toward the use of all reinforcing substances. These are the long-term trends in our society. Marijuana and cocaine and some other drugs are bucking that general trend because they are "new" substances going on a different track at the moment. In the future, they will be incorporated, I think, into the larger downward trends. There is reason, in the long-term, for modest optimism.

In the future, we as a nation are going to do much more to distinguish between youthful use of drugs and adult use.

This is one of the most important distinctions that we must make. It is a tragedy to treat 12-year-olds like we treat 20-year-olds when it comes to the use of alcohol and tobacco and other drugs. A national commitment to protect young people from exposure to drugs is overdue. There is a clear movement toward a differentiation between public use of drugs and private use. You can see this with tobacco. I think we will see it with alcohol. It will also turn up in all drugs, I suspect. We are also seeing a dramatic distinction between occasional use and regular use or daily use. You may be surprised, as I was, to find that large majorities of the population, including the youth population, which is the most heavily drug-using segment of our population, are strongly opposed to regular use of any drug. Whereas youth have a relatively casual attitude about using marijuana once a month, the attitude toward daily use of marijuana or daily use of alcohol is strongly negative even in our youth population. We are going to see a lot stronger attitudes about driving while under the influence of alcohol and marijuana and any other drug including prescription tranquilizers. All these trends I have been describing are easily discerned in the national opinion surveys that are conducted annually by The National Institute on Drug Abuse (NIDA). These trends characterize *all* age groups.

Let me now say a few words about some of the directions in which I see the drug abuse field going. It is important to realize that the drug abuse field, unlike the alcoholism field, is new. We lack the sense of tradition that exists in the alcohol field. It is interesting to note the ages of the people who are in the drug abuse field. At the ripe age of 43, I am an old man in the drug abuse field, but I am right in the middle of the alcohol field in terms of age or maybe a little bit on the young side. There are great advantages available to the drug abuse prevention field from using the wisdom that has been reinforced in the alcohol field.

By far the most important lessons drug folks can learn is how to cooperate with and support the AA tradition. The tradition of self-help, I think, is the most important single thing that the drug abuse field needs for the future. We also can learn something useful from the incredible ambivalence and the complicated relationship the alcohol field has with the distinction between abstinence as a goal and moderation as a goal. Just to deal with those issues is very important for the drug field. The drug abuse prevention field has been totally committed to the abstinence goal.

One of the most important events that has occurred in recent years in the drug field is something that you in the alcohol field are already familiar with: the emergence of respected members of society who come forward and talk about their problems with drugs. Partly because respected members of society tend to be older and most of the people who have drug problems are younger, this has not happened before. Also drugs have the extra stigma of being illegal.

The courageous statements by Betty Ford, talking about both her alcohol problem and her drug problem, her pill problem, have made a tremendous contribution to the drug abuse prevention field that those of you in the alcohol field may not fully appreciate. The fact that Mrs. Ford, who is one of the most respected members of our society, could talk frankly about the insidious way she became dependent on drugs is an enormous step forward. This dependence was a result not of her seeking thrills. It grew out of her attempts to deal with chronic pain. This dependence grew, not out of some antisocial statement, but out of the seduction of the drug experience. Her message was very powerful.

Again, largely following in the footsteps of our colleagues in the alcohol field, we in the drug abuse prevention field can look forward to much more involvement in the mainstream of health care systems.

The stability of the drug field over the last decade and the talented people who have been recruited into it have given the field that previously had very low legitimacy, a lot more legitimacy.

Of those factors, the main one, I think, has been the very exciting work in the field of endorphin research. The discovery of the body's own morphine-like neurotransmitters suggests that it is not purely accidental that we have a vulnerability to opiate dependence. In fact, there are specific cells in our brains that are uniquely responsive to opiate drugs and to the body's own opiate-like substances. This has opened up a whole new area of biomedical research that promises to be even broader than the issue of neuropharmacology. It includes how we feel pleasure and it helps explain for the first time, such surprising phenomena as the working of acupuncture, for example, and even the placebo effect. This exciting area of research is almost certain to produce a Nobel Prize for medicine and physiology within the next few years. This too will contribute dramatically to the legitimacy of our field.

I speak with some hesitancy about the newness of the drug abuse prevention field and also about the need for legitimacy simply because there was a noble, distinguished tradition of excellence in the drug abuse field at the Addiction Research Center in Lexington, Kentucky. It was a small but important beacon of excellence for many years prior to the growth of this field during the last decade. From that beachhead of excellence have grown many fine programs, including the entire National Institute of Mental Health. After World War II, the Institute grew out of the Addicition Research Center. The first involvement of the federal government within mental health was dealing with opiate dependence after World War I.

The drug abuse field is going to become increasingly committed to prevention. Prevention probably will never receive the level of federal funding that treatment now receives, for a variety of reasons, but the overall investment of our society will be much greater in the prevention area than it has been in the past. Prevention has been handicapped in the drug abuse field because it has been so difficult to think about what a comprehensive prevention *program* would be, for this county, or for a state, or community. The costs and the varieties of prevention programs appear to be almost limitless. In an era of budget restrictions, this is not a good time to think about open-ended costs and poorly defined programs.

We are now realizing that there are some distinct modalities in the prevention field that need to be funded and supported. The first is *information*. We are still not providing adequate information to the people who really need it. Of all the things that we are not providing people right now, I think the major missing ingredient is the emphasis on the health hazards of marijuana use. One of the big mistakes we have made in the marijuana area is to be caught up in the legal aspects of marijuana use. The whole decriminalization-legalization issue is largely a symbolic issue. It is a red herring that has distracted us for several years. We need to get back to providing good information about the health consequences, the very disastrous health consequences, of marijuana use.

We need to help people think through issues about deciding to use or not to use various drugs. *Education* is the second modality of drug abuse prevention. We need to educate people about values and feelings especially. I wonder, for example, how many young people are aware of the fact that of those people who have ever used more than a pack or two of cigarettes in their lifetimes about two-thirds spend most of their adult lives addicted to cigarettes. I wonder, when a young person thinks about whether to smoke cigarettes or not, if he realizes that the odds are two out of three that if he smokes more than a pack or two of cigarettes, he has a 65 percent chance of spending the bulk of his adult life addicted to cigarettes. I don't think people have that information. I also wonder whether young people who are thinking about alcohol consumption have figures about the risks of alcoholism. I rather doubt it. I doubt that they realize that roughly 10 percent of the drinkers in the country become alcoholics and even more have a serious alcohol-related problem during their adult lives. For most of us, a 10-percent risk sounds like a serious risk to run.

The third modality of drug abuse prevention is *alternatives*. This, I think, is the most complex and the most difficult modality to program, but it is clear, whether it is on a community level or a family level, that it is important for us, especially when dealing with young people, to provide them with attractive alternatives not just to drugs, but to drug-using life styles. These alternatives should be attractive and constructive and widely available for the young people.

The last modality of prevention, the fourth area, is *early intervention* or identifying people who have problems with drugs early and providing them with services to get them back into the mainstream and out of a drug-using cul de sac.

There are many ways in which we can build together and in which we can benefit greatly from the synergism of alcohol and drug programs. I believe that those of us in the drug abuse prevention field can learn much from the alcohol folks, including the whole concept of industrial-based drug programs. The best way for the drug field to go is to simply join in and take advantage of the tremendous progress that has been made in the alcohol field in industry and in many other areas.

On the other hand, I have learned that it is important to maintain some distinctions and not to simply lump all these problems together and call them "chemical dependency programs." Lumping everything together is often done at the cost of programatic coherence and the ability to communicate to the public in general and to those in need of help specifically about what one is doing. Those who are planners at a state, county, or federal level often see great similarities between various kinds of behavioral problems being treated. However, unless they understand the importance of a clear rallying idea, a clear identity to a problem, in terms of the development and support of that program, I think we are going to suffer greatly from the lumping and blurring that now appears to be in vogue.

Finally, we hear talk about our fields of drug and alcohol abuse as second class; as less distinguished than the other medical or the social services areas. That reflects the stigma that unfortunately is still attached to drug users and alcoholic people as well as to those people who help them. If we step back a little bit from our struggles we will realize that rather than being behind the rest of medicine and social action programs, we are substantially ahead. The evidence I would ask you to think about is this: How can our national health status best be improved? You are immediately struck with the fact that any improvement in the health care delivery system, such as improvement of treatment of heart attacks, for example, or improvement of treatment of cancer is unlikely to substantially influence the average life expectancy in the United States. There are not as many gains left as there were at the turn of the century when the conquest of infectious diseases was the top priority. We often hear the figures that American life expectancy has doubled in the twentieth century. I wonder how many of you know that the doubling of the life expectancy is almost totally a result of reduced *infant* mortality. The life expectancy of the average 40-year-old in the United States has increased only about three years since 1900. The total increase in life expectancy that we tout so often is the result of infant mortality reduction. If you do look, however, at what we can change in the future that will improve our health status, the quality of the life of our people, you quickly come to realize that the area where the impact must be made is not in infectious diseases, it is not in sanitation, it is not in vaccines, it is not in treatment of heart attacks, or cancer. The great gains during the remainder of the twentieth century will be in *prevention* and specifically in the area of life style change. Potential progress lies in the area of choices we make as individuals about how we live. That is true for cigarettes, true for alcohol, true for drugs, true for our diet, and true for exercise in our society. All of the areas where we have any substantial hope in the next 30 years of improving the health status of the country relate to our life styles. The only one exception perhaps is the environmental area, but even that is a distant second to life style issues. When it comes to changing life styles, the problem is people's choices. How do we change ourselves and how do we help others change? If you want to talk to a doctor who is frustrated, talk to a doctor who sees his first alcoholic patient, gives good advice, and finds that his patient does not take it. The doctor does not know what to do. In medical school, they do not train us about life styles and how to change them. We give advice on diet: our patients do not take it and we do not know what to do. Our fields of drug and alcohol abuse prevention have developed expertise in helping people change their life styles so that they can do more for themselves. So that people with problems can help each other. So they are not dependent on expensive, long-term health delivery systems. All of the models that the medical field, and for that matter, the social services, are groping for, already exist in the drug and alcohol fields. All of the techniques that we use everyday are applicable across the board in all these "new" life style areas. So perhaps it is time for us, rather than feeling that we are a bit behind, to stand proud and recognize that we are substantially *ahead*. We can begin making contributions to these broader areas based on our hard-won knowledge. I am proud that I have spent the last decade working with all of you in these fields and I look forward to keeping at it for several more decades.

Discussion

Chaired by Robert DuPont, M.D., the panelists who participated in this discussion were Robert M. Derman, M.D,

Chief, Psychiatry Service, Veterans Administration Hospital, Northport, New York; Walter Donheiser, Ph.D., Coordinator of Drug Abuse Programs, South Oaks Hospital; Alexander J. Licastro, M.D., Family Practitioner, Old Bethpage, New York; Thaddeus J. Murawski, M.D., Director, Office of Professional Medical Conduct, State of New York, Department of Health; and Wayne Rothwell, C.S.W., Director of Drug Abuse Programs, South Oaks Hospital.

Dr. Derman:

At Stony Brook we conducted surveys in 1974, 1976, and 1978 on drug use among the undergraduates. The figures are rather startling. Though the students themselves have tried in very high proportions most of the significant drugs that are abused, 95.6 percent of the kids had tried alcohol in all three years studied. The real question was raised about the 4.5 percent who hadn't. Again 70 percent of the kids had tried marijuana and that is a fairly consistent figure. The issue, however, is how many of them really use it with any degree of frequency; what is surprising is that very few do. Even in 1974, when 6 percent of the youngsters reported they had tried heroin or another narcotic, nobody used it three times a week. So that one has to look not so much at what an individual has tried but the pattern in which it is used, the likelihood that it is going to be influential in their lives. I agree with Dr. DuPont that by the time these youngsters reach college, I think the pattern has been set; these are, by and large, successful people. The real issue is one that I hope that others with more experience will address on the panel and that is the junior high and high school problem.

Dr. Donheiser:

I would like to make some remarks on what we see here in the teen-aged drug abusers who need to be hospitalized. (There is a kind of personality configuration in polysubstance abusers.) They will take anything. Some have a chemical of choice, but some will take about anything that comes along. One thing we have noticed is that they tend to ingest chemicals to cope with life; to cope with feeling, love, hate, anger, frustrations, fear. Almost any experience will evoke the need to ingest some kind of chemical substance.

Another part of this configuration or syndrome is the behavior problem. They almost all show some kind of behavior problem. Poor impulse control, what I might call a disingenuousness attitude; that is, a tendency to try to get over, even if it is completely inappropriate. This is what we call the *dope fiend mentality*. Of course, manipulation is a great part of this. They manipulate people and situations in order to get their impulses and needs met. Most of them appear to have kind of a passive-aggressive orientation toward life and a philosophy that is strongly hedonistic. Live for today. "I have the right to do whatever I want to do with my body and with my personal life—no matter what the consequences." They tend to have a disregard for the future. Live for today, don't think about tomorrow.

There is a marked inability to own, that is to possess, their feelings, and to feel comfortable and at home with these feelings. Underlying a great deal of this, we seem to find a feeling of object loss; that is, the feeling of loneliness or unrelatedness to people that tends to be accompanied frequently by a very low self-esteem; an incomplete or distorted body image; unreachable or unrealistic goals or ideals; almost a perfectionistic orientation with the feeling that, if I have to be perfect, which is in fact impossible, then why should I bother trying at all as there is no sense in trying the impossible to begin with.

Along with this self-destructive trend, there is an overriding tendency to get into trouble, to engage in antisocial behavior and thrill seeking. "Devil may care." Maybe most important of all, dope fiends have a great deal of difficulty in establishing new object relationships; that is, becoming deeply involved with people, particularly new people in their lives. Sometimes we talk about this as a lack of object constancy. When a person is not there to meet their needs, that person, for all practical purposes, does not exist for them. They go on to the next person and the next person in order to try to extract whatever it is that they are trying to get. In treatment, they have a great deal of difficulty in establishing a therapeutic alliance because of the difficulty in object constancy.

As one of the speakers said today, the patient will come in and talk with you for many sessions and just when you feel that you have got the thing in hand they revert back to whatever behavior problems were shown before. We find that, in order to do anything with these young kids who are polysubstance abusers, we must almost forceably stop their acting out. You must give limits and structure to them. As soon as the acting out is stopped, they begin to experience the warded-off feelings and then you can begin to work with them therapeutically. The feelings begin to suddenly whelm up inside them and with the help of peer pressure, they start to verbalize. This is when you feel you have a therapeutic hold on the patient.

Dr. Licastro:

I'd like to give a brief summary of my own personal background in the field of drug abuse and then perhaps you will see where my involvement started. After I finished my residency in internal medicine in 1966, I was asked to start a clinic for multiple drug users. Within several months, the clinic was inundated with referrals from almost every sector—from alcohol to barbiturate overdose.

Several months after, the county created the Nassau County Drug Abuse Commission, which was responsible for the initiation and development of various modalities in the treatment of drug abusers.

At this point, as we went from school district to school district, professional and nonprofessional Commission members began to get the idea that we are not here at the right school. We should have gone across the street to the ghetto areas because drug abuse was not here. Statistically, it was interesting because the prominent drug abusers and users were in the so-called better middle class- or upper middle-class white neighborhoods. The number of youngsters involved in drug abuse and violence was frightening and prompted us to start a detoxification center that I was asked to run as the medical director. Well it was like the little Dutch boy with the dike. You treated five or six abusers and suddenly another hundred clients appeared. Within weeks I began seeing the same clients requesting treatment after having returned to drugs. It was obvious that an epidemic had already started that was quite severe. I will not attempt to relate the story of our problems in trying to convince the school authorities of the severity of the epidemic. That is now ancient history.

Several years later, Topic House was started for youngsters who were primarily involved in the family court, in acting-out behavior, or who had been referred to us from various legal and medical agencies in the county. They were usually 14 or 15, up to 16 or 17 years old. We groped our way through untried and new treatment approaches with very able psychiatrists and several well-informed lay people. It became evident shortly that the problems were much more deep-rooted than drug abuse. Drugs were not the problem, only the symptom. One could remove the majority of these youngsters at the beginning of their drug usage or abuse with a tried and proven multifaceted approach without difficulty. For example, we would see 100 clients and 80 would do well with intense, closely supervised treatment: the apparent quick therapeutic response. I suppose this goes back to what the former speakers said—the object feelings or systems. If one had an individual who lacked formal training or exposure in the formative early years of life in the moral (society) question of right and wrong, the probability of even partial limited success in treatment in patient rehabilitation was minimal. Their values and standards, as formed in their early years, created a negative attitude toward their lives and society, which neutralized all known therapeutic approaches at that time.

Therefore, if one were to question the therapeutic success of Topic House at that time, it would have appeared to be limited; though a successful therapeutic level of 30 percent was much higher than other modalities at that time, with success rates of less than 5 percent.

With the high failure rate for hard drug users at that time, however, we finally decided to start a Methadone maintenance program in Nassau County in November 1970. I was asked to initiate, supervise, and become medical director of the clinic. I had a very select group of patients which, due to their primary and sole use of heroin, presented as a rather uniform and predictable group of patients. The true heroin-addicted individual was easier to deal with because they lived and functioned with almost identical values. Within two to three years, there began to appear in this select group, the polydrug user—"the garbage head." Suddenly and dramatically the clinical picture changed. It was my impression I was now seeing youngsters, who at a very early age, probably 7 to 10 years old, demonstrated inabilities in dealing with society, family, or peer group pressures. Whether these problems were pathological, personality defects, or responses to situations within the home or their own peer group, they responded by using drugs. However it started, many youngsters began to self-medicate themselves in order to deal with their environment or inner conflicts. As an example, one can easily rationalize that to function in a stressful social setting, it is necessary to have several alcoholic beverages. Suddenly it doesn't have to be a party for one to use alcohol; any excuse is valid. Shortly it is easy to believe, why not boost it with a little "pill or two." Somewhat similar to what we as adults would do in having an alcoholic beverage, saying as we fix a drink, "I can't relax after work without a drink and I can't enjoy myself at a party without a drink.'' Many times statements being made to no one in particular, but rather out loud to ourselves.

With parental credibility in question, youngsters verbally attacked their parents, and so increased the generation gap. The ensuing drug addition or drug usage was described as paramount, but as we have come to discover, the preceding problems were much more important.

Therefore, we saw youngsters who were not in terrible need of true psychiatric help. What we had were nonfunctioning family units, involving parents and youngsters. In response to this need we attempted to increase counseling; other supportive services were provided to individual patients and family units. But funding became almost impossible at times. As has been society's response in the past, a quick solution was sought—Methadone maintenance. It was sold by various segments of society as the panacea to our drug problem. It was easier to think of it in that sense than to see where the real problem was. The real problems, as indicated briefly, required extensive funding, and there was no nationwide leadership. Methadone maintenance was easy; a patient was hospitalized, detoxified, and then titered to a dose of daily Methadone; that they required no other treatment was the thinking at that time.

The error in that thinking and planning need not be gone over at this time, history has done that for us. That therapeutic direction—give *all* drug users Methadone—prompted me to leave the drug treatment world in 1975. Time has supported my beliefs and views, and I only hope that history will be a guide for us all, in urging we direct our treatment efforts toward the individual and his functioning in all aspects of his environment; be it family, social, or whatever.

Dr. Murawski:

It is difficult for me to understand why I am on this program because I am the policeman who sees the end result of drug usage in physicians. We see the end stage for the physician when he has run the gauntlet and injured patients. Ours is nothing but a punitive measure rather than trying to do something about the drug problem itself. So, nevertheless, from our limited experience it certainly shows that it is not only the physician who rejects the idea that he has a problem or who has a defense mechanism against it, but we find that the families themselves do not try to help. And, sadly enough, the medical profession is well aware of the problems in their colleagues but they make very little attempt to do anything about it, to get their friend into some kind of program, or to caution him that he may be running into some difficulty. These people will not help. By the time they come to our attention (these people are loners) they are in a great deal of difficulty with society. As you know, there is a great public clamor to do something about all of these "bad doctors" and so they wind up in our lap and, as I say, we have to be punitive about it.

The other distressing thing is that when we attempt to talk to lawyers who defend these physicians and tell them that there are other mechanisms to help rehabilitate physicians other than going through the administrative process, we are told that lawyers will defend them to the end because this is their right. So the end result many times is license revocation. There has to be early identification before you can do anything with these physicians. They can be rehabilitated and I think they can be reprogrammed. But you have to get them very early. Second, in the younger physician population that comes to our attention, if we dig deep enough in the history, we find this history of drug usage dates back well into medical school. It may very well lead back into high school and even earlier. In the elderly physician, it seems that the drug problem arises from some sort of physical ailment, a sickness, a physical injury.

The goal of the Board for Professional Medical Conduct is to rehabilitate a physician and get him back in the mainstream of medicine. But there is a great deal of difficulty in physician reentry into the system. In other words, will the hospital accept him back on the staff after he has gone through a drug problem or rehab program? Will the community accept this physician treating patients again knowing that he was a drug user at one time? At times you may have to reprogram a physician, and by that I mean you might have to encourage him to change his specialty. You may have to persuade him to no longer give anesthesia, to no longer do surgery, to get into other areas of medicine. With the paperwork society that we have, there are enough jobs for physicians to do so that they do not particularly have to have direct patient contact. Or, have the physician work in some sort of protective environment where he doesn't have all the pressures of working alone, trying to make all the decisions by himself.

Now the only approach that the State Board for Professional Medical Conduct had made recently was to have the legislature enact a temporary surrender of license statute. This means a physician who has some particular problem—it can be a physical ailment, senility, or a psychiatric, alcohol, or a drug problem (providing there has been no third-party injury, meaning that we have not received a complaint from a patient that some harm was done)—can approach the Board, temporarily surrender his license, and accept the terms of the Board as to what he has to do to rehabilitate himself. After fulfilling certain obligations, whether it is physical therapy, psychiatric therapy, a detoxification program, or whatever, he then comes back to the Board and establishes that he is fit to go back to practice. At this point the Board can recommend to the Commissioner of Health that his license be restored and get him back in the mainstream of medicine. But again, I would like to emphasize one point. By the time they come to a disciplinary board, it is the end stage and it is extremely difficult to help them.

Mr. Rothwell:

Dr. Weisman asked a very interesting question today: "How many people feel that an alcoholic is responsible for his drinking?" Some people raised their hands and he said, "Well, I caught you." Being a process person, what happened was that I was two questions ahead of him. My questions were: How many of you think he is not responsible, and, how many of you don't know? Five years ago I could have sat here and told you what I knew. I don't know what I knew then, anymore.

It has always been my feeling that drug abuse, any kind of drug abuse, is symptomatic of a number of problems and that you will find some underlying disturbance—neurotic, psychotic, whatever it may be. I view drug abuse as a self-medicating process. I used to believe in this very strongly and still do; however, now I have questions in terms of something Dr. DuPont raised today and which I have talked to some physicians about, the endorphin theory of morphine addiction. There may be some evidence that drug addiction is biochemically related. There may be some people who are more or less predestined, or who have a condition for which they may need or find a great deal of solace in certain kinds of drugs. So, I am not sure any more.

What impressed me most in the conversation we heard this morning with Dr. DuPont were his feelings about prevention, early intervention, and industrial drug programs. I will start with the field of prevention. I have been in this business for 10 years, actually 16. Six years of it I spent on the other side of the curtain. I was a drug user. In the 10 years that I have actually been working with people who are polydrug abusers, we have tried a number of approaches to prevention—everything from going into the schools and giving kids valid and factual information about what will happen if you use drugs, to the kinds of things you see on television now about what they are doing in the jails, like *Scared Straight*. All of it in the beginning seems to give good results, but in the long run I have found that it doesn't.

Early intervention is probably the focus that I see as the most important one at this point. In young people today there are things that you can see in their attitude, things that you can see within their value and conduct systems, things that you can see in their behavior, that give you a handle that there is the possibility there will be problems later. What you are going to actually do in terms of early intervention is another question. I am not really sure. I have seen a number of approaches used. I have worked in community drug programs and still do. I have worked with inpatient groups. It has been my experience that the right person connects with another person at just that right point in time and the object relationship that Dr. Donheiser was talking about before is established at that given point in time. They manage to actually gain, for the first time, socialization and habilitation. I have seen people come into our program here or in an outpatient setting, who for five years on and off, have absolutely no movement at all. Suddenly they come in one day and that relationship begins; or they come in and they have another therapist and that relationship begins. I am not exactly sure what it is but I am sure of this: it had to do with their own motivation. It had to do with their own need and their own want to be helped. People don't get help by some magical thing that we do in an office or on the street or in their homes or to their family or to them. They get help because they decide one day, as somebody said this morning, they're "sick of being sick." They are sick of being identified and labeled that way and they are sick of the consequences of their behavior. So what happens is they come to a realization that, I really need some help with my life and I am willing to kind of surrender it and let somebody else try and help me with it. I'm willing to listen and try to put into action some of the ideas that we have come up with together.

I grew up in the mid-1960s, began to use drugs when it was popular, about 1964. I started with marijuana. I had a typical progressive history. Marijuana, barbiturates, amphetamines, eventually into heroin, and finally methadone. I was involved in criminal justice systems. I was involved with the Department of Drug and Alcohol Addiction. Eventually I was in Topic House. After I left Topic House, I was among a group of people contacted by Dr. Carone and Dr. Krinsky here at South Oaks. Through some of their patients they learned of the successful treatment of addicts by former addicts. They decided to institute a similar program here at South Oaks, combining the therapeutic community model with a psychiatric approach. Essentially what we do on a day-to-day basis is to implement a treatment plan that is humane and supportive but at the same time structured. This takes place in a family-type environment where we try for socialization and habilitation. We try, through interpersonal relationships, to establish, perhaps for the first time, object constancy, people being friends with other people and understanding the consequences of their behavior.

Audience:

If we agree that drug abuse is symptomatic of other internal or extenal problems, in the past five years how much have societal pressures added to this self-medication process?

Dr. Donheiser:

What I was trying to imply was that one is not necessarily a cause of the other. It seems to be a syndrome or a package and we see this as a cluster. The drug addiction is not necessarily the result of these problems but these problems seem to go together. I don't think your average adolescent shows the degree of poor self-image that we see in these kids. I think it is a matter of degree rather than anything else. But, how do we identify the 1 kid out of 10 who is going to become an habitual drug abuser when all 10 have tried the same drugs? Just as with alcoholics most of us have had a few drinks from time to time and only a certain percentage of us become alcoholics. This is the critical question and I don't know what the answer is. I don't know how to pick that 1 kid out of the other 10.

Dr. DuPont:

Some of you may be familiar with George Vaillant's follow-up study of a group of Harvard College graduates about 40 years later. It is called "Adaption to Life." He asked the question, who became an alcoholic and who didn't? He debunked the idea that anyone could predict on the basis of what happened to these people as kids who were going to become the alcoholics. He showed the protocols of the people up to college age to a group of experts and asked, O.K., now pick who will become the alcoholics. They were just absolutely random, they could not pick out the future alcoholics. After the disease alcoholism is started, you can "see" all kinds of factors in the person's past and draw a lot of conclusions. It is not, if you know this perspectively, quite so obvious. This gets back to the point that Mr. Rothwell made about early intervention. In the early stages of these processes, whether drug dependence or alcoholism, people seeking treatment are labeling themselves. You can be very effective in targeting at that point when that process is under way even in early stages; whereas, when you go to the whole population it may be more difficult to pick out the future alcoholics and drug-dependent people.

Audience:

Prevention, which to me means education, has to start very early, and it must be on a national level. Ten years ago Wayne Rothwell came to our school to talk to our junior high students, and the impact he made was incredible. I still talk to college students who remember him. The kids have to see it and be among the young people who have had it, who have known about it, and can teach them. If we as adults try to do it, as doctors, as teachers, as psychiatrists, it doesn't go. The kids have to know about addiction just as they learn in kindergarten how to draw and how to spell.

Dr. DuPont:

It is fascinating to me that as experts and as a nation, we have come full circle, in a sense, about scare tactics. One of the great lessons of the early 1970s in the drug field was how bad scare tactics were. We are now in the process of relearning the usefulness of scare tactics. It is interesting how much easier it is to scare people straight than to talk straight about all the subtle issues known and unknown. When you really get down to what it is you are trying to say and try to get some declarative sentences put together, you often come back to scare tactics. This is the problem today with the government's drug and alcohol abuse prevention messages. They sound like mush, because you have got so many committees to go through and so many points of view to reflect. Every statement is qualified beyond meaning to the public.

Audience:

How about educating those who serve as role models? It may be too late for some of these kids, certainly those who have reached their late teens and early 20's. But if we can get at the parents of relatively young children, let's educate them.

Audience:

I am an industrial alcoholism counselor and we find today more dual-addicted people. We don't get the garden-variety type alcoholic anymore. It seems that everybody we get is addicted to more than one drug. We can put them into a rehabilitation center, but somehow it seems that they always come back and get back into the drug scene again. What about this problem of dual addiction?

Mr. Rothwell:

The area is a gray area. Once again, it has to be individualized. If certain behaviors, certain criteria, certain attitudes are there, our kind of approach is successful. If they are not there, it is not successful. We also don't work well with certain kinds of people and we know this.

Dr. DuPont:

I have found it helpful to think about the life style, about the quality of life of the person. Once you focus on that issue—I am talking about after a person is in a treatment program for drug or alcohol problems—then a lot of switching back and forth between substances can be dealt with fairly comfortably. The impact on the quality of life of the person, in his human relationships with other people, is more similar than the pharmacology of those drugs would suggest.

Audience:

The scare tactic that we used originally was to bring ex-addicts into the schools to rap with the kids, and we thought, great, they'll see. But their attitude was, well, look they made it after all, I don't have to worry. That was the response we got. I was a teacher, now I am a social worker in an industrial setting, and we don't know what works. What we are trying now with high school students is a human relations tactic; getting kids together in groups from all different kinds of communities just to talk. These are not kids who are abusing drugs. As Dr. Licastro said about the "me" generation, there is a tendency away from groups, and a focus on "what can you do for me?" I think that that is the problem that has to be addressed.

Dr. Licastro:

Different strokes for different folks. There are certain people who benefit from certain types of treatment and there are certain people who don't. You are trying to find one answer to all problems by saying, remove the drug, remove the alcohol, and the person is going to be a nice person. But again, I believe when you remove those factors, only then do the problems *really* come out. Then you are dealing with a whole slew of problems that are varied in their origins, cause, and effect. The industrial counselor who spoke before is probably seeing the youngsters I saw 14 years ago. One cannot expect a youngster of yesteryear, having gone full cycle with the traumatic experience of those years, and now expect a "well-adjusted" individual without hang-ups or negative experiences. It is going to be a slow process, which must be continued, with increasing force and support in those extremely difficult and important years of everyone's life. And, as difficult to accept as it may be, we must brace ourselves and accept the realization that there will be failures of individuals.

Dr. DuPont:

Both the industrial and the school setting hold enormous promise in terms of both treatment and prevention. You have criteria for adequacy of performance that are clear-cut; for example, attendance. It's a very simple matter, either you show up for work or school or you don't show up. Also, productivity can be relatively easily measured. Feedback, so that the person in treatment has information about his performance that he can see is clear-cut, makes an enormous difference in terms of being able to communicate clearly about what the problem is. That alone does not solve the problem, but I think the potential in both the areas of the school programs and industrial programs is tremendous. It needs to be exploited much more than it has been in the past.

Audience:

I work in a local jail and our feeling in the jail is that you see the same people over and over again. The same people over and over again and with the same line and the same manipulations. Our viewpoint, almost 100 percent, is that it is a hopeless process. They will be let out and they will do it again.

Dr. Murawski:

Since I have been involved with professional conduct I have been trying to keep numbers and many times these numbers hurt us because people say you have not done enough. Everybody talks about what is going on but how many can come up with good, hard data to support their claims? I think we ought to come up with some statistics and descriptive data. The A.M.A. is saying 7 percent of the doctors have problems with drugs or alcoholism. Gee, in a state of 35,000 practicing physicians with the network that we have, I would like to know where this 7 percent is.

Dr. DuPont:

It has been my experience that the number of physicians who are involved in what might be called promiscuous prescribing is relatively small and relatively easily identifiable. It is just a tragic situation when the only way to stop a doctor from prescribing amphetamines and Methadone is to prosecute him for a felony and send him to prison for 15 to 45 years. A physician in Washington, D.C. is now serving such a term. If we had any kind of statute to pick up his license he could have been saved from that dismal, but well-deserved, fate.

Anyhow, the point is that overprescription is relatively easily identified both at the pharmacy level and the physician level. What we need is an aggressive program, which I gather you have in New York, to identify unusual prescription habits and then to actively pursue it. It really isn't much of a problem for the average doctor. I don't believe that is where the problem is. The large amount of "prescription" drugs in illicit use comes from a few doctors who are writing thousands of prescriptions for controlled substances, and essentially selling them. What we have to do is pursue those people. A large, but unrelated, problem exists in overly casual use of psychotropic medicines by well-meaning physicians and patients. To deal with this problem we need education not law enforcement.

Audience:

I would like to revert back to the analysis of prevention. I think that indeed we can expect very little in the way of health improvement from personal health services. Most of the improvement will come through environmental health services and changes in human behavior.

I am the Commissioner of Health for the County of Suffolk, and we do have preventive programs and yet I cannot help feel a sense of disquiet. We have not had very signal successes in approaching those conditions and diseases that require changes in behavior, partly because we sometimes run countercurrent to larger societal trends and changes, and partly because we spend very little money in finding out.

We should change the balance of dollars. For example, in this state alone, if one talks about general health, we spend about 1 percent of the state health dollar on prevention, and the rest on treatment. I dare say if you look at drug treatment programs throughout the United States, you would find very little going into prevention. The next thing I would urge, because I don't believe things are unknowable, is that we ought to foster and support more epidemiological and more behavioral research rather than put all of our emphasis in the direction of laboratory bench research. I think that would give us some basis for sound preventive programs.

Dr. Donheiser:

It would be very helpful if there was some kind of control over the advertising industry, both in terms of alcohol advertising and in terms of the type of advertising that fosters impulsive and hedonistic kinds of behavior without any thought of consequences.

Dr. Derman:

I would like to sound a warning about all this good intention prevention. We have lived through, some of us, the 1930s and the 1940s when the government took a strong hand in terms of telling us what drugs were like, what they did to us, what they did to our bodies. In effect, I think we lived through some very devastating misinformation that turned off the people in the 1950s and ultimately turned around the people in the 1960s. I don't think the government is in any real position to tell us what is good and what isn't. I don't want to see a time when the government is running the radio stations or the television stations, because they may be determining everything as well as drug use. They're going to determine how I use my car in a very short time. I think you ought to think twice before you start advocating a massive prevention campaign run by the government.

Dr. Licastro:

As an internist, I deal with many elderly people who have chronic illnesses. If a diabetic goes into acidosis, I say, you should increase your insulin; for a congestive heart patient, take an extra water pill. If the patient is a drug user, however, we in general medicine say, you are a drug user, you failed once, you are a terrible person, goodbye; for an alcoholic, a return to alcohol evokes a statement indicating patient failure since abstinence is the only therapeutic response we accept. It is really the only area in medicine where we don't accept failure, remission, or noncompliance in the treatment of a chronic illness. We must accept, without reservation, that drug abuse is a chronic illness, which many times is progressive despite intense and accepted treatment regimens; that it has its "roots" in one's early life and, according to some, even during one's intrauterine life cycle.

Audience:

Mr. Rothwell said that early intervention is important and I agree. Do you have any suggestions for developing this early intervention? Where do your referrals come from? How supportive have the schools been?

Mr. Rothwell:

How successful you are going to be with a school depends on what the school's attitude is. Much of the time, what you are going to find is that the school people are caught in a bind such as: if the child is in our custody and if the child says something to you, or you identify him as a problem, then we have to contact the parents. We are struck with this situation and we have to give them all the information that is a professional violation of confidentiality, but, in terms of the law, is a requirement. So you get caught in a bind. If you want to work in a school, you can't do treatment. The mandate, I think, is three visits. I know this in terms of the school drug programs in Nassau County that were set up in May 1977, so it may have changed. The mandate was that you could see the kid three or four times; after that you had to refer out. You had to refer to the local community agencies or to some other form of treatment. The treatment actually worked in the schools. In terms of prevention, I have been advocating the peer model for the past 10 years—using the peer model under direct supervision. No one seems to hear me.

Audience:
   Are you talking about peer counseling in groups?

Mr. Rothwell:
   Yes. A guided group is a valuable treatment modality. It can be done supportively in early intervention to perhaps turn some things around with the kids. You are providing those role models that were talked about before, and you are providing a lot of support and friendship. You are providing all of this when you take some of your good students in the school, and you activate them and get them involved with kids who feel that loneliness and that sense of uniqueness, and get them to share. You have to get families involved as Dr. Licastro suggested. You have got to do the whole nine yards. Of course, there are many problems—politically, financially, and particularly emotionally, on the basis of the family saying, "Hey, I don't want my kid in this." "My kid may want to, but I don't want him to." "Who are you to tell

me this about my kid?'' ''I think it is your problem.''
Professionals in those systems often are afraid to tell the
truth. We're afraid to confront the problems for fear of the
repercussions.

Dr. DuPont:

I'd like to give you a little research background. The
ethic among young people is basically antidrug. The way kids
get into a prodrug life style is to form small subgroups
around drug-using ethos. The dominant ethos is still very
much antidrug. Anything you do that encourages bringing
the drug-using kids back into the general stream in their peer
group is going to reinforce a drug-free life style, and is going
to negate the drug-using life style. The only exception to that
is the ethos that the kids have of, ''You do your thing, I do
mine.'' In other words, the one thing that inhibits kids from
getting more aggressive about that is, ''It's your body, your
decision.'' Once you can get across the idea that we all share
in this—that I have a responsibility for you and you have a
responsibility for me—then you free up these more positive
attitudes. This is one of the reasons that larger schools, for
example, have somewhat more drug users than smaller
schools. The obvious reason is that in the larger school the
students have an easier time forming subgroups around
''deviant'' attitudes like drug use than they do in smaller
schools where it is harder for them to break off and find a
peer group to support a drug-using life style.

Audience:

I have worked in the drug field for almost 15 years, and
it is sad to see that the problem remains and is growing. I too
am very interested in prevention because obviously with all of
our treatment programs, we have not been able to stem the
tide.

Dr. DuPont:

Part of the problem in prevention is to think through the
issue of what you really want to buy. When you say you want

to work with the first and second grades, when you start programming that, you start running up just astronomical costs. Unless you are talking about a very small number of people, it becomes difficult to program direct person-to-person prevention services. From my point of view, what is needed more than anything else is a comprehensive programmatic framework that takes the whole wide spectrum, not just the early grade school youngster but also the middle-aged prescription drug user, the whole range of need for prevention. Frankly that has not happened.

The budget people are much more interested in an idea if they can see clear evidence that the target population is of manageable size, if you have a program that you know how to run, and if you can demonstrate the cost effectiveness of the program. I think if you could show, for example, with hard data, that you had a program that was more effective at reducing specific drug problems, prevention would sail very quickly. The reason you run into trouble is because the people in the Bureau of the Budget ask questions that the prevention people cannot answer. Until they can answer those questions, I don't think prevention is going to get the money.

However, prevention folks know they have the politics on their side. For those who are looking at which way the wind is blowing, it is blowing toward prevention. It is just a matter, I think, of being able to capture and harness that energy and turn it into specific, affordable programs. This is one of the key tasks of the next decade. It is going to take more than good wishes and heart to solve this problem. It is going to take some very tough programmatic thinking, including the ability to say "no" to some attractive ideas.

Your target audience is the person in your budget office. If you can convince him, you are going to make it.

Dr. Derman:

There are not enough follow-up studies to give you effective data. What in essence is happening is that you have programs that are like hobby horses. People ride in for a few years, and then the hobby horse is put together with a new coat of paint, and moved down the block a bit. There are no outcome measures. One can see the youngsters drift from one place to another over the years. I think until we have a sophisticated way of determining outcome measures for therapeutic modalities, we have no right to ask for additional funding. This is something that has been neglected by all the agencies involved.

Dr. DuPont:

Compared with other social service and health fields, there has been much more commitment to data in this field. There are clear criteria to measure success. For example, reduction of arrest rates, increase of employment, and reduced drug use are three objective measures.

The dominant study in follow-up of treatment was done by Saul Sells of Texas Christian University; he has followed up a random sample of the first 47,000 admissions to federally funded drug abuse treatment programs between 1968 and 1973. The follow-up time is now an average of about eight years after these people were admitted to programs. The problem with that data is the embarrassment of the *positive* findings. The drug use is so reduced— particularly the heroin use—in that population as to make you wonder about it. Ninety percent reduction in daily use and 75 percent in "current use." Employment is increased about 10 percent, crime is reduced by about 50 percent. That is a national study, involving some 300 clinics all over the country. The hard data are available.

Audience:

The answer to that is that they are eight years older and as they grow older, they settle into "the straight life." Your answer may be that no program worked, it was just a matter of getting older.

I think we all believe that peer groups work. But we have very few statistics that tell us exactly what causes change and, unfortunately, the people who do the follow-ups usually are the same people who set up the programs. I don't say that they are not telling the truth, but they do have a skewed attitude.

Audience:

More and more we hear how available drugs are in the schools and how children know exactly where to go to get these drugs. What are we doing as far as cutting off the source? What are we doing about the pushers who prey on young children in the schools?

Dr. Licastro:

In Nassau County, most of these children started with drugs found in their own homes. They went right to the medicine chest for Valium, Seconal, and every pill they'd heard about on television or in their daily living. They have grown up believing today's motto: "Take a pill and you can cure all your ills." Yesterday's, today's, and probably tomorrow's drug abusers found their beginning in their own home. The youngsters themselves are the pushers.

In tracing back over the pages of the story, the source of all drugs has always been a difficult question to resolve. Let me tell you again, it is not the man on the corner with the black hat and coat up around his neck who is selling drugs to our children. It is not! If a youngster wants to use any drug, there must be a predetermined set of circumstances, be it internally, or in his external setting or environment, that helps create the setting for drug use. The easy availability of drugs in itself alone is almost never sufficient for someone to use that substance. One need only to realize the large number of people who are exposed to the same availability who never use any drugs.

Audience:

There are many of us who are worried about the availability of drugs in the schools and who see people coming around the schools who really should not be there.

Dr. Donheiser:

Some of the drugs they get around the schools are coming fresh out of boxes—from Lederle, Smith, Kline and French—not through doctors. I don't know where they come from but there they are.

Audience:

I can't believe the majority of it comes from the homes. I believe it is pushers who prey on children.

Dr. Licastro:

The children aren't that innocent that they sit there and say, "Oh yes, please give me the pill, I don't know what it is going to do."

Audience:

But they don't know any better!

Dr. Licastro:

We spend a great deal of time teaching, instructing, and showing our children to be very sophisticated, mature, and responsible; to cross the street alone, to make decisions involving careers, jobs, money. We threaten or voice opinions that drug use and abuse is wrong. However, we fail to see how our actions speak with greater force and credibility. I do not think it's necessary at this time to repeat the well-known many-time-used cliches. It is our actions, our behavior that is incredulous to the youngster; and prompts his questioning our actions. It is our failure, as grown mature individuals, to look at our behavior and to change those that are harmful to our person or as models to our children, that helps in delaying changes that are necessary to stem the tide of drug abuse in our society at all levels.

Dr. DuPont:

I would like to comment about what we call in policy terms, supply reduction. This means programs and policies aimed at reducing the availability of drugs. It is one of the most interesting and important areas in the drug abuse field. There is an enormous societal investment in the area of supply reduction and much of it is remarkably successful. I will focus on heroin addiction because for much of the last 10 years that is what I have spent my time working on. We have had remarkable success in reducing the availability of heroin in the United States since 1972. Largely heroin availability has been reduced by activities outside the United States; first with Turkey stopping cultivation of opium and then later stopping supply from Mexico.

There has been about a 50 percent reduction in heroin overdose deaths in the last two years in the United States. That is a significant reduction. We should, as a nation, feel good about it. Heroin is now for sale in the United States at about 200 times the price it would be if we had no supply reduction activities. One of the best and most objective measures of the success of supply reduction is the price, because the price is going to reflect supply and demand in the market. The fact that heroin costs 200 times the price it would cost if it were openly available is an objective measure of the constraints put on the supply of heroin in relationship to demand. The irony is that the more we inflate the price through successful supply reduction efforts, the more incentive there is to the production system to supply it! That is a dilemma to which there is no solution—absolutely none. It is just one of the fascinating dilemmas that one runs into in drug abuse prevention.

As to what happens in the schoolyard, I agree with you that we have restrained ourselves far too much in terms of dealing with the local dealer, the local seller. But let us not delude ourselves; the·local seller is our child. O.K.? So when we go after him (or her) and we send him to jail, which I support, let us remember that he is our kid. The local schoolyard seller will not be the kid from some other neighborhood. We should get tough; I think that a lot of us have been much too restrained in the past. The kids would benefit from a new hard line. The big dealers are something else. I am talking about who is selling it on the schoolyard. It is our own students, our own kids, and we will have a high price to pay in our own families. I think that is one of the reasons we haven't done it.

Audience:

We can't lose touch with the fact that the person who needs drugs for whatever reason, even if you take away the drug pusher, is going to find his distortion of reality elsewhere, be it alcohol or something else that is available. You really have to start from the other end, from the psychological aspect. You can't lose touch with that.

Dr. Derman:

There's another line to that. For example there are some people who enjoy committing muggings, even though they are now drug free. They can't give up the life style that went along with drugs despite the fact that they no longer obtain drugs. I think it is a very important distinction that you make, because in many instances what we are going to be dealing with are people whose behavioral styles are not really going to change, and their life styles are not going to change. Perhaps the drugs are secondary after all.

Audience:

I laugh every time I walk into our county jail because we sell highly dangerous drugs in little cellophane packages. There is a machine that dispenses them. Alcohol, go to the local package store and get all you want. What troubles me on a very basic level is that if I like alcohol and you like cocaine, my drug is legal, but your drug isn't. It strikes me as government by caprice.

Dr. Derman:

Why don't you try obesity or some of the other things that we are dealing with. If you are going to be a fascist on any level you can be a fascist on all levels. What I am saying is, you have got to be very careful how you start regulating the people of this country, who are one of the least regulated people in the world. I am not sure where you are going to stop when you have done it. I remember a day when we used to put abortionists in jail. I am very much afraid that the guy who is dispensing Methadone today is going to be tomorrow's criminal or scapegoat.

Audience:

You can go to your local tobacco store and you can go to your local alcohol store and buy all this stuff that is responsible for terrible deaths and terrible miseries.

Dr. Donheiser:

You can buy glue in a hardware store.

Dr. Derman:

One cause of bleeding ulcers in this country is aspirin. What do you do, stop selling aspirins just because someone is going to have a bleeding ulcer? It is not by removing the substance that we help people. What we must do is educate them, make them aware.

Audience:

I am going back to my feeling that we start when they are little kids. How would you suggest that we educate them?

Dr. Licastro:

Maybe we should start with the parents. Maybe we should start *before* they become parents. You cannot regulate social, moralistic change—the social revolution that has gone on in this country and this area in the last 10 years, aided by our own failure to discipline ourselves, has contributed more than most of us are willing to accept.

Audience:

I have been in the industrial field for 31 years. When we started, we had 15 employees. Now we are up to 350. I have to say that we have grown much faster in numbers than we have in knowledge. I guess we are like the parents who say, it's the other kid who does it. But we are being faced with the drug problem in our company and I would like to know what resources there are for personnel people who must deal with this problem.

Dr. DuPont:

The National Institute on Drug Abuse does have occupational programs, just like NIAAA in the alcoholism area. That would be a place to start to get some information about occupational drug programs. Write to National Institute on Drug Abuse, Parklawn Building, Rockville, Maryland 20852.

Audience:

You can get a tremendous amount of help in these areas by contacting other firms, other personnel departments. We have found the most effective tool is job jeopardy. We give a troubled employee the choice of coming here to South Oaks or to some place of his own choice, or going out that day with his last paycheck. We haven't had one man who has gone out with his last paycheck.

Dr. DuPont:

That point is important. There has been a kind of stridency to some of the comments today that may mask a much more shared opinion about what needs to be done and what we can do. I think that comment brought us back, from my point of view, to the fact that people reasoning together and sharing some humanistic values can often contribute to solving even very difficult and devisive problems.

Audience:
Dr. DuPont, there now seems to be some fairly conclusive evidence that marijuana is harmful.

Dr. DuPont:
The most important event in the marijuana field in recent years was the NBC documentary, "Reading, Writing, and Reefer." There are several excellent things about that program. One, it separates adult marijuana use from child marijuana use. It also examines the health problem of marijuana use.

Let me quickly tick off the areas of major concern. The first is intoxication. As with alcohol, the primary disabilities in the alcohol area are those related to intoxication, chronic and acute intoxication, ranging from driving, to work performance, to interpersonal relations, to studies, to everything else. The primary characteristic of somebody who stays high on marijuana is that he doesn't care; use of the drug reduces his constructive anxieties. That whole knot of issues dealing with intoxication is a primary concern.

In addition, the major active ingredient of marijuana is tetrahydrocannabinol (delta-9-THC) which stays in the fatty tissues of the body, unlike alcohol, for example. It is like DDT, it accumulates in the fatty tissues, including the brain and the reproductive organs. Thirty percent is still in the body one week after ingestion. It tends to build up in the body—even if a person smokes marijuana only once a week—in the course of time. THC has been shown to have an effect on cell division, including DNA synthesis, and produces profound effects, including effects on cellular immunity.

The male sex hormone, testosterone, is depressed by marijuana use. Marijuana has a very bad effect on the lungs.

Chronic bronchitis is a regular occurrence in frequent use of marijuana. Laboratory studies show that human lung tissue exposed to marijuana smoke shows more precancerous changes than similar tissue exposed to tobacco smoke. A recent study comparing marijuana smokers with cigarette smokers, in terms of the effect on their lung capacity, showed that it took 17 tobacco cigarettes to equal the effect of one marijuana cigarette. That shouldn't be surprising to anybody if you think about how marijuana smokers smoke. They pull the smoke in and they hold it in their lungs. Marijuana smoke has more tar and known carcinogens in it than tobacco smoke does, so it hardly is surprising that it has this effect. There is now good evidence that the effects of marijuana are much more harmful than people have thought.

We must get away from trivializing marijuana use. We must see it as a serious issue, very much the way we are growing to see the decision to use cigarettes or alcohol as serious. Unfortunately, many young people in this country still believe that their decision to use marijuana is a trivial issue. What happens with scientific evidence is that one study goes this way and one study goes that way. People tend to feel that there is nothing to any of these studies. What this really means is that this is the way science is. Before you put the final nail in, it is going to take years with a lot of conflicting casting about. But none of the studies shows marijuana safe. The "best" that ever happens is to find an inconclusive result. I don't think any marijuana researchers feel that this stuff is safe, especially when it is used regularly. In 1971, people really thought that the dominant pattern of marijuana use was to use it once a month. Nobody in 1971 expected that 11 percent of today's high school seniors would be smoking marijuana every day! That is a totally unexpected finding and this whole concentration on heavy marijuana use is just a fantastic development. Did you know that *daily* marijuana use is now *twice as common* as *daily* alcohol use among high school seniors?

Dr. Murawski:

Being an old environmentalist in air pollution I just want to make a more general comment. If you smoke anything with a high tar content, you are going to have lung problems so it doesn't necessarily have to be marijuana.

Dr. Derman:

What about the studies on the 30-year use of hashish?

Dr. DuPont:

There are three studies: Costa Rica, Greece, and Jamaica. The total number in all three studies was 120 people. The people who were chosen for these studies had to be healthy. The researchers studied only people who were healthy. If you took 120 cigarette smokers and picked out only healthy cigarette smokers and tried to decide how bad the health effects of cigarettes would be, I don't know what you would find. Again, I don't want to overstate the case against marijuana. I don't think the marijuana epidemic is the end of our society. But my concern is that there has been a tragically false impression that the stuff is harmless. That is a *very* dangerous idea to have around.

Chapter 3

AN OVERVIEW OF
COMPULSIVE GAMBLING

Robert L. Custer, M.D.*

Gambling has the power to generate a pleasurable challenge for about two-thirds of the adult population who make wagers of one kind or another each year. The vast majority of these gamblers are nonpathological gamblers, that is, social gamblers. A very small number of these gamblers make a living by gambling—the so-called professional gambler.

The antisocial personality who is involved with gambling (the one most frequently confused with the compulsive gambler) does so as a method of stealing and just as one aspect of his overall lifelong career of crime.

Then there is another group of gamblers who will risk their reputation, their family's security, their life's savings,

*Robert L. Custer earned his M.D. degree at Western Reserve University. He is a diplomate of the American Board of Psychiatry and Neurology in Psychiatry. Dr. Custer is the Chief of the Treatment Services Division of the Mental Health and Behavioral Sciences Service at the Veterans Administration Central Office in Washington, D.C. In addition to initiating an inpatient treatment program for compulsive gamblers at the Brecksville VA Medical Center, Brecksville, Ohio, in 1972, he is the Medical Advisor to the National Council on Compulsive Gambling and has worked closely with Gamblers Anonymous and Gam-Anon.

their work, their freedom, or their safety on the turn of a card, a roll of the dice, or the legs of a horse. Gambling for them is not recreation, not a job, not a part of a criminal career. They are the pathological gamblers, the compulsive gamblers.

Compulsive gambling is the type of disorder in which there is a progressive increase in the preoccupation and urge to gamble. This results in excessive gambling that eventually reaches the point where it seriously damages the gambler's personal, family, and vocational life. The cardinal features are emotional dependence on gambling, loss of control, and interference with normal functioning.

Historically, the United States has been a gambling society. The pendulum has swung many times between permissiveness and prohibition. Actually, the 13 original American Colonies were largely financed by lotteries, as were Harvard, Yale, Princeton, Brown, Dartmouth, and Columbia. George Washington, Benjamin Franklin, and Thomas Jefferson staunchly advocated lotteries as a means of raising public funds. Although we are now in a permissive phase, public attitudes remain essentially judgmental and moralistic toward compulsive gambling and the compulsive gambler. It seems moderate risk-taking is more socially valued in our society than caution; but caution is infinitely more acceptable than reckless risk-taking. Perhaps another way of expressing our value is that we admire a risk-taker who wins and reject a risk-taker who loses. It is not that they are naive, they know that the odds are against them; they have a deep passion for gambling. They love the "action." This is epitomized in the classic saying of the compulsive gambler: "Do you know what the next best thing to gambling and winning is? Gambling and losing."

Our society has been confused by this apparently mindless and irresponsible behavior with its staggering loss of money, waste of one's efforts, extreme deprivation to the family, and damaging effects to the community. The simplest way to deal with this baffling behavior is to reject and punish. During the past few years, however, there has been a perceptible change in attitudes that the public is beginning to approach this perplexing problem less emotionally and more realistically. The origins of this change began with the rise of Alcoholics Anonymous, which provided the framework for the development of Gamblers Anonymous in 1957.

Then, five isolated but distinct developments in the early 1970s began to interrelate and lead to social changes. These developments were (1) the development of the National Council on Compulsive Gambling, Inc., (2) the inpatient treatment program initiated by the Veterans Administration at their Brecksville, Ohio, Medical Center, (3) the Commission on a Review of a National Policy toward Gambling, (4) the draft of the APA DSM-III which included compulsive gambling (as pathologic gambling), and (5) the rapid growth of legalized gambling in the United States.

By the late 1970s, these developments directly led to Maryland being the first state to legislate funds for treating compulsive gamblers; the bill proposed by Senator Williams of New Jersey for the establishment of a National Commission on Compulsive Gambling; the courts' recent decisions that have begun to recommend probation, treatment, and restitution for compulsive gamblers; and the listing of the DX Pathological Gambling (312.31) in the International Classification of Diseases, Ninth Edition, Clinical Modification (ICD-9CM). All of these developments indicate that our society is beginning to temper its attitude with thoughts of helping, rather than punishing.

If the lesson learned from the recent international study on alcoholism applies to gambling problems, in that "total consumption is a common denominator for problems," then the data revealed by the National Gambling Commission are significant. In 1960, Americans wagered about $5 billion through legal commercial channels, by 1974 this figure had grown to more than $17 billion, and in 1978 it was $21 billion.

Who gambles? In 1975 the Survey Research Center of the University of Michigan conducted a nationwide study of people age 18 and older. The study showed gamblers to be:

- 68% of males and 55% of females
- 62% of white and 52% of nonwhite
- 73% of the 18-24 age group
- 69% of the 25-44 age group
- 60% of the 45-65 age group
- 23% of the 65 years or older age group
- 51% of those with incomes of $5,000 to $10,000
- 74% of those with $15,000 and over incomes
- 41% of those who did not graduate from high school
- 79% of the college graduates
- 80% of Catholics
- 77% of Jews
- 54% of Protestants

The Michigan group also estimated that there were 1.1 million probable compulsive gamblers and 3.3 million potential compulsive gamblers. They indicated that availability of gambling seemed to increase the risk of becoming a compulsive gambler and that legal gambling facilities seem to stimulate illegal gambling. Thus, the recent surge of interest in legalized gambling as states attempt to find new and possibly painless sources of tax revenues, likely are stimulating illicit gambling and compulsive gambling.

At present, there are only three known facilities, all in the Veterans Administration, that have special program expertise in treating compulsive gamblers; similarly, very little research has been done in this area. However, these programs appear to have answered two basic questions that Gamblers Anonymous had previously answered: (1) it is a unique problem and (2) it is treatable.

Pathologic gambling is synonymous with the more commonly used term, compulsive gambling. It is likely that both terms will be used for many years to come: "Pathologic gambling" will be used more by the scientific community and "compulsive gambling" will be used more by the lay groups. One should feel free to use either term as long as it is clearly understood that they are interchangeable. The reason the scientific groups prefer the term "pathologic" over "compulsive," is that compulsions are the behavioral component of the obsessional state in which a person finds his or her abnormal behavior alien and attempts to resist it. If this element of resistance is not present, the use of compulsive should be avoided. These gamblers, classically, admit that they enjoyed gambling even though the consequences may be dreaded. The pleasure component, from a strictly scientific viewpoint, moves the disorder into an impulsive area and out of the compulsive area. Therefore, "pathologic gambling" is a more appropriate scientific term, since it is solely descriptive and is not based on any assumptions about conscious or unconscious motivations.

Causes

The study of excesses of gambling behavior has had contributions from a number of disciplines. Psychoanalysis has contributed insights. Also learning theory has provided much insight as have anthropology and sociology. These different theoretical frameworks are compatible and can provide a level of understanding that goes beyond any one of them.

The first serious efforts to understand the behavior of compulsive gambling were made by psychoanalysts who sought to shed light on the intrapsychic conflict and psychodynamics of the individual gambler. The first paper of any significance to explain gambling from a psychoanalytic viewpoint was that of Ernst Simmel in 1920. He saw gambling as an effort to gain "narcissistic supplies" such as food, love, comfort, and attention, which the gambler felt had been denied him. Wilhelm Steckel, in 1924, saw the gambler as a child in play and the adult gambler as one who has regressed to childhood. Steckel felt that gambling mania arose out of man's desire to avoid work. Next, was Sigmund Freud's "Dostoevski and Parricide." He saw the murder of Dostoevski's father as a completion of the wish of Dostoevski, plus the source of his burden of guilt. Freud extended Steckel's observation on the relationship between gambling (play) and sexuality. Freud wrote, "The passion for play is an equivalent of the old compulsion to masturbate." This provided the framework for Edmund Bergler's central thesis stated thus: "I submit that the gambler is not simply a rational though 'weak' individual who is willing to run the risk of failing and moral censure in order to get money the easy way, but a neurotic with an unconscious wish to lose."

Theodor Reik saw gambling as more than just substitute behavior. He believed that the gambler addressed to fate the question that unconsciously torments him: will I be punished or forgiven for masturbating?

Some of the last significant psychoanalytic contributions are those of Ralph Greenson and I.E. Galdston. Greenson felt gambling was a neurotic defensive function to ward off feelings of impending depression. Galdston stated, "In my experience with compulsive gamblers, I find no support for Freud's formulation that compulsive gambling is a replacement for compulsive masturbation." Strangely, psychoanalysts stopped writing about compulsive gambling at this time about 20 years ago. Then began the contributions of behavior theories.

Ivan P. Pavlov's work led to B.F. Skinner's theory and research in operant conditioning. Skinner demonstrated the powerful influences of intermittent reinforcement. He sees the pathologic gambler as the victim of an unpredictable schedule of reinforcement.

Theories about sensory deprivation have contributed much about the optimal arousal in a given organism. R.H.

Thompson observed that, "It seems much more likely that solving problems and running mild risks are inherently rewarding or, in more general terms, that the arousal will always act so as to produce an optimal level of excitation." Berlyne stated, "Some degree of uncertainty can serve to make life less dull." Gambling certainly has this quality of "uncertainty."

Anthropologists such as Bronislaw Malinowski and A.L. Kroeber saw the influences of uncertainty reflected in magical thinking. Among gamblers, similar behavior is rampant.

Sociologic approaches deal with availability of gambling, the social stresses and rewards, the limited options to the gambler as losses accrue, peer pressure, and modeling of behavior.

Physiologic theories have not been presented but one is impressed by clinical cases of gamblers that fairly consistently show constitutional factors such as their brightness, high energy level, hyperactivity, and high tolerance to stress.

The experience of the Brecksville treatment program has been that only 10 to 15 percent of the compulsive gamblers show a neurotic configuration. Most were not guilt-ridden, masochistic megalomaniacs who strive to lose. Many had prolonged winning experiences. Many showed a sexual adjustment that was frequently satisfactory until late-stage deterioration compounded pleasure in *all* areas.

Compulsive gambling is the least studied of the significant psychological disorders. The causes are still obscure but it probably represents a confluence of numerous psychological, social, cultural, and even biologic factors.

Course

In contrast to alcoholism and drug abuse, compulsive gambling is a "drugless" disorder. However, the compulsive gambler typically describes the overall effects while gambling as similar to the effects of a stimulant-tranquilizer analgesic, simultaneously. Although it has been said that compulsive gamblers gamble to escape or avoid reality, there is evidence that they may be doing this more in a manner that creates an acceptable form of reality to them—a fantasy world in which they can feel important, challenged, powerful, influential, and respected. The need for these feelings likely reflects the very areas in which the gambler feels inadequate.

The compulsive gamblers present rather typical premorbid personality traits, uniform patterns of development and progression, and predictable complications. The Veterans Administration clinical studies have shown typical adolescent traits: superior intelligence, vigorously competitive, a hard worker, an unusually high energy level, inclined toward being overly generous, good school performance, and little or no delinquent behavior. This individual likes challenges and seems attracted to stimulating situations. Boredom is poorly tolerated. They seem to thrive on excitement. They are not relaxed. They resist parental discipline whenever possible, mostly to avoid the inactivity of restrictions. They relate well to peers.

Petty gambling with peers usually begins in early adolescence. Significant gambling begins about age 17 for males and age 25 for females. However, gambling can begin at any age. It also occurs in either sex but predominantly in males. All racial and socioeconomic backgrounds are involved. However, it appears that it is more common in Catholics and Jews and in those with Irish, Italian, and Oriental nationality backgrounds.

The time interval between onset of gambling behavior and loss of control varies from 1 to 20 years with most occurring after 5 years from onset of gambling. A few feel they are "addicted" with the first bet.

The compulsive gamblers admitted to the Brecksville Medical Center inpatient treatment program always had a preferred form of gambling, but usually used many forms. The preferred forms were about equally divided among five types: flat horseraces, harness races, card games, dice, and sport betting. Rarer types were bingo, jai alai, dog racing, the stock market, and the lottery.

The course of the compulsive gambler can be roughly divided into three phases:

Winning Phase

In the early phase (winning phase), the individual gambler frequently has a history of a substantial win, initially or very early in his gambling career. This usually occurs prior to the legal age in a legal gambling facility. They continue to win frequently and become enthused and excited prior to and with gambling. The amount bet is steadily increased but huge increases are not typical during this phase. Gradually, they begin to bet more frequently. The gambler is pleased with his winnings and tends to splurge or squander this added money to impress others. During this phase, winning continues as knowledge of gambling, odds, and risks is quickly developed. At this point, the gambler is a skilled gambler, can stop and still has control, but does not want to stop what is so enjoyable and profitable. There is rare borrowing at this stage since winnings are usually adequate.

This phase may continue for months to several years and, typically, ends with a substantial big win that approaches an amount nearly equal to or exceeding the gambler's annual salary at that time. The winning, and particularly the big win, establishes in the mind of the compulsive gambler that it can happen and could happen again, and could be even larger. They also see this as the solution to any financial problems. Also, it is enjoyable and requires little planning or effort.

Losing Phase

This winning phase heralds the end of the first phase and the beginning of the second phase (losing phase) when an attitude of optimism about winning has become a classical part of their style. They brag frequently about their wins, and gambling is always on their mind. At this time, their gambling behavior begins to lose more and more of the social context, and they begin to gamble alone. After the big win, the amount of money bet significantly escalates with anticipation of still larger wins. Then, they encounter a losing streak that is difficult to tolerate. Their winning pool is quickly depleted since they are betting much more heavily. Then, they draw upon sources of money they may have earned, saved, or invested in order to get even. Losing is intolerable. They must get their money back. They begin to chase, that is, they bet more in order to recoup losses. It is a pattern that wise gamblers consider the cardinal sin of gambling. The compulsive gambler who has developed an irrational optimism disregards this principle. He bets heavier, and more frequently, and with a sense of urgency that seems to diminish his betting skills. This in turn leads to more losses. The search for money intensifies, and bond cashing, cashing in insurance policies, and legal borrowing begins. Borrowing is a new experience for the compulsive gambler. It has for him the quality of a gambling win—money promptly available with no effort required. The future payments required are thought to be no problem since gambling will provide the money.

Again at this point of heavy borrowing, there is a substantial increase in the amount gambled. The once skilled gambler is now a much less skilled gambler who is betting more. The intent is to repay the loans as quickly as possible in order to prevent the family from knowing. Covering up and lying about gambling behavior become increasingly more important. The gambler becomes very ingenious at giving excuses to his spouse and employer. But he "knows" that a winning streak is inevitable and only the next bet away.

The gambler begins to lose time from work and his productivity diminishes. The family sees less and less of him and when he is at home, his attention to family needs and problems is not forthcoming. As the inattention (preoccupation with 'gambling) increases, family and work problems increase. The relationship with the spouse, who feels betrayed, deteriorates markedly once lying is exposed. Wins do occur periodically through this phase, but the winnings usually represent less than what has been borrowed. At these moments, only the most urgent debts are paid but most cash must be held in reserve to insure prompt return to gambling activity. Although there are ups and downs, the compulsive gambler continues to lose ground. The fervent wish of the gambler is to have even larger wins, to pay off debts, and to have a large money reserve to avoid borrowing again and allow for uninterrupted gambling.

The pressure of the creditors increases and threatens the secrecy and safety of the compulsive gambler. Bills must be intercepted or explained. The family deprivation of basic needs leads to alienation from spouse and parents and children. As legal borrowing resources are exhausted, the risk of illegal borrowing emerges. This begins first with the bookie, later with the loan shark. Eventually, these pressures lead to a critically dangerous financial state in which the gambler must have a large sum of money or be in danger of injury, divorce, loss of job, imprisonment, or death. At this point, the gambler gives at least a partial confession and pleads for money from parents, spouse, or in-laws. Invariably, this money is provided in order to bail the gambler out of his predicament. With the bailout, there is either an open or tacit agreement to stop gambling. The bailout seems to be particularly damaging since it does not allow the compulsive gambler to assume responsibility for his own behavior. It is similar to the big win which again encourages unreasonable optimism, and it creates an illusion that nothing bad can ever happen to him. Any cessation of gambling is short-lived.

Desperation Phase

The first bailout marks the end of the losing phase and the beginning of the third phase, desperation phase. Several bailouts are likely to occur during the third phase with a steady erosion of genuine concern, which progresses to alienation as those family members loaning the money see no repayment *and* continued gambling behavior. The characteristic of this phase is another marked increase in the amount of time and money spent gambling. There appears to be a state of panic caused by the knowledge of large amounts of money owed, the desire to repay promptly, the alienation from family and friends, the adverse reputation in the community, and a nostalgic desire to quickly recapture early days of winning. Thus, the gambling increases at a frenzied pace with the belief that a huge win would repair all of these problems. The optimism that this win will occur continues but is beginning to wane.

The striking characteristics of this phase are the consuming intensity of gambling, and the apparent disregard for family, friends, and employment. Under this pressure, the once skilled gambler is now the stupid gambler. Losses of available money, without credit for loans, leads the gambler to increased risk of further illegal loans and nonviolent crime to obtain money. Some are much more likely to also become involved in a dishonest maneuver (scam) to obtain money from other naive and unsuspecting gamblers. Bad check writing becomes the chief technique to obtain funds. They rationalize this illegal behavior on the basis of full intent to repay what they have taken. They are stimulated by the image of repaying their skeptical creditors. Surprisingly, a few compulsive gamblers are able to continue their employment or business throughout this phase. They seem to have the energy to pursue two full careers simultaneously. The compulsive gambler is never a relaxed person but the restlessness, irritability, and hypersensitivity at this stage increases to the point that sleep is disturbed. Eating is erratic, and life has little pleasure. Even in this late stage, there are still occasional significant wins but this only leads to heavier gambling and heavier losses. Then the world of the compulsive gambler comes crashing down. They are physically and psychologically exhausted with a feeling of hopelessness and helplessness. They are heavily in debt, alienated from everyone, on the verge of divorce, and welcome nowhere. One-fourth of them are about to be arrested. Depression and suicidal thoughts and attempts are fairly common at this time. It is not known how many complete suicide. It is at this time they see only four options: suicide, imprisonment (others controlling), running, or that they seek help. They still have the urge to gamble.

Treatment

The initial problem for the helping person is frequently a problem of recognition. The compulsive gambler may admit being depressed and state it is due to threatened losses such as a spouse leaving, loss of a business, huge losses of finances, and/or legal complications. Gambling may not be revealed. If the problem of compulsive gambling is suspected, however, the spouse can quickly verify the origin of these problems. More commonly, the problem will be admitted. A typical excerpt from an initial interview is, "I feel emotionally beat—and I've thought seriously of committing suicide. My family has given up on me. I've borrowed thousands from my parents. I've written a letter to tell them how sorry I am. I tried to explain that I didn't want to gamble, but that I couldn't control it."

The suicide risk must be determined and is usually easily done by direct questioning about their past suicidal behavior and present feelings and intentions. Inpatient treatment is indicated for the management of the suicidal patient, particularly one who has no family support system. The exhausted compulsive gambler who can't see any way out of serious predicaments, who is isolated due to family alienation, and who might be showing signs of emotional decompensation, may need a protected environment. Some may be desperate, not suicidal, but are on the verge of committing a crime as an irrational attempt to resolve their financial problems. Thoughts or intentions about this option need to be explored in all cases by the helping person. In essence, many cases truly represent psychiatric emergencies.

The observations of the staff at the Brecksville Treatment Program revealed that if the compulsive gambler had just stopped gambling, it was not at all unusual for symptoms of headache, abdominal pain, diarrhea, cold sweats, tremor, and nightmares to appear for a few days after admission. This may represent withdrawal symptoms or may be due to sleep starvation. Irrespective of what might produce these symptoms, they respond favorably to sleep, a rigid type of routine, a regular diet, vigorous exercise, ventilation, and reassurance.

With the initial interviews, the gambler will describe gambling behavior that has come to dominate his life, leading to multiple serious consequences, in a way that almost appears to be bragging. The interviewer is frequently told that no one could have had such troubles, such debts. One is struck by the inability of the gamblers to control their behavior, in spite of the consequences, and apparent ineffectiveness of either reward or punishment to modify it. They usually say they want to change but don't know how. One learns that they also have little hope that change is possible. The family history will reveal problems of alcoholism or compulsive gambling in the parents in about one-third of the cases. The surprising part of the history is the absence of antisocial behavior as a child or adolescent, with a good school and work performance.

There are four rather consistent defensive postures that the gamblers will take. The therapist would be wise to confront these issues early:

1. They believe that lack of money is the problem.
2. They expect an instant or miraculous cure.
3. They cannot conceive of life without gambling.
4. They see complete restitution of debts or stolen money as desirable but impossible.

The concrete problems the compulsive gambler faces, aside from the gambling behavior, typically are spouse-family disruptions, immense debts, demands from creditors, loss of a job, alienation and isolation, threats of the loan sharks, the legal entanglements.

Simultaneously, the problems of dealing with the hurt, the fear, and the angers of the gamblers are made difficult when it is realized that there seems to be a "feeling aphasia," in that they have considerable difficulty recognizing or verbalizing their feelings. However, they are usually quite articulate and can recognize feelings in others. This makes them particularly good candidates for group therapy, especially with other compulsive gamblers having the same "aphasia" and abilities.

Strengths of the gamblers make rehabilitation efforts much easier than initially expected. One can capitalize on their high intelligence, industriousness, high energy level, competitiveness, and desire for independence.

These traits are particularly effective in reestablishing vocational activities. Vocational efforts are natural and ego-syntonic avenues for these enterprising individuals. Work becomes a time- and energy-consuming activity that substitutes significantly for their drive to gamble. It is not uncommon for them to secure two or three jobs. This eases their financial pressures, but probably more important, it is a more constructive channel for their energy and provides them with a sense of regaining control of their lives.

The basic goals of treatment are: (1) no gambling, (2) *full* restitution, and (3) assistance in developing constructive substitutes for gambling.

Compulsive gambling is a chronic, long-standing disorder which requires long-term care, and in view of the fact that it is impulsive behavior, and that stress stimulates impulsivity, it is wise to develop a system that will provide access to someone who can reduce tension at any time it might develop. A therapist needs to have a high degree of availability to the gambler. This is one of the advantages of GA. Numerous members are skilled, available, and willing to provide help. The more people are available to "talk down" the compulsive gambler who feels driven to gamble, the less of a chance for relapse.

Relapses (slips) must be watched for and treated promptly so that areas of the gambler's life that stimulate gambling can be understood and dealt with appropriately. Marital counseling and assertiveness training are usually quite valuable as protective measures against relapses.

Gamblers Anonymous (GA) and Gam-Anon

The first meeting of GA was held in Los Angeles, California, on September 13, 1957. Since that time, GA has grown steadily and there are now hundreds of such groups throughout the world.

GA is a voluntary fellowship of compulsive gamblers gathered for the sole purpose of helping themselves and each other to stop gambling and stay stopped. The only requirement for membership is a desire to stop gambling. There are no dues or fees for membership. Membership is never solicited. Direction to GA can be given by anyone, but this help is given at the request of the compulsive gambler.

GA represents a program for living without gambling. It is a program of 12 suggested steps that provide a framework of hope, structure, and friendship from those who have lived the program and successfully adapted to life without gambling. GA is effective because it undercuts denial, projection, and rationalizations. They demand honesty and self-responsibility. They are not only nonjudgmental but provide the hope and affection that are so essential for the person whose life seems ruined and chaotic.

Many compulsive gamblers can recover fully with GA alone, with no professional help. Others like to utilize both approaches. A few seem to need professional help for some time before they are able to accept GA. One of the chief advantages of GA is that they willingly provide an understanding person who knows the pain the compulsive gambler has but never wants to admit.

Gam-Anon is a fellowship for the families of compulsive gamblers that began in New York City in 1960. Families of compulsive gamblers have found living with a compulsive gambler to be a devastating experience. With Gam-Anon, they learn to cope with problems in the face of disaster. They hope to and do accomplish many things: understand the compulsive gambler, help GA, learn to talk out feelings, deal with guilt feelings, do things for others, set priorities, learn to plan and meet some of their own needs. It is a place where they are understood.

Female Compulsive Gamblers

There appears to be a rising number of female compulsive gamblers. Several reasons for this seem apparent. Money is the "drug" of the compulsive gambler, and women's ability to earn and borrow money has been increasing. Also, they are now freely admitted to gambling facilities. As in alcoholism, society is more negative toward the female compulsive gambler. This forces the female to delay reaching out for help. Another delay factor is that the breadwinning husband will repeatedly bail out the female compulsive gambler, much to her detriment. Another hurdle for the female is that the husband is not as likely to give emotional support to treatment as by attending Gam-Anon. Still another hindrance to the female's approach to treatment is her difficulty in integrating into male-dominated GA. Currently, female compulsive gamblers are estimated to comprise about 20 percent of the nation's compulsive gamblers. However, they represent only roughly 4 percent of the GA membership.

Conclusion

In conclusion, the compulsive gambler has been considered as weak, bad, or different. Some politicians deny their existence. Many courts condemn them. The legal state gambling programs profit from them. Many professionals don't know about them. Loan institutions continue to be easily duped by them. Loan sharks bleed them. The families unwittingly encourage them. The compulsive gamblers, themselves, aid in their own destruction. The role of the helping person will be frustrating and challenging, but with knowledge, skill, and understanding, it can be, most certainly, rewarding because the compulsive gambler can and does recover.

Chapter 4

PRESENTATION BY THREE COMPULSIVE GAMBLERS

Gambler A:

I am a compulsive gambler. I haven't found it necessary to make a bet now in more than 17 years.

That's the basic way we would start to speak at any of our meetings. GA does not deal with any cause. We just deal with symptoms. We take people who have a desire, for whatever reason, to stop gambling and we work with them and encourage them to work for themselves. We are not crusaders; we are not do-gooders; we are not doctors. We are nothing else but compulsive gamblers. Some of us fit into the compulsive gamblers category, and some of us are pathologic gamblers as Dr. Custer stated. But we are all working together as individuals and working together collectively.

Our meetings are not conducted by professionals nor do we have any professional help at the meeting level. We have people from every walk of life, from every form of occupation, and from every educational level, financial level, marital level, and criminal level. We are completely heterogeneous. We are not a social club, yet we do socialize. We are not a financial club, and yet we do show people how to plan their financial futures. We try to help the compulsive gambler and the family of the compulsive gambler in any way we can. That means standing next to them in court. It means going with them by the hand to the shylock, going to I.R.S., any way possible, except by lending money. In other words, we are not interested in bailing them out. This brings to mind one possible conflict. Will the legal and the medical societies, through their efforts to help, form a type of bailout for the compulsive gambler? I don't know the answer. I don't know if California, all of a sudden, said, a compulsive gambler won't be put in jail for bad check writing, will that be helpful? I don't know. As Dr. Custer stated, we do strongly encourage everybody to pay back everything that they owe. We do not subscribe to bankruptcy. That is not one way of paying back.

Gambler B:

Ladies and gentlemen, I am a compulsive gambler. Or, more appropriately, as Dr. Custer says, a pathologic gambler. I am 54 years old, been married 19 years, I have three children, three cars, two dogs, two mortgages. Pretty average on the face of things for most middle-class people. That is where the similarity ends.

I am a product of a broken home. I have one sister a few years younger who over the last 20 years has become a compulsive seven-day-a-week bingo player. My pattern of gambling started when I was about 13 years old. I don't think I was truly compulsive at the time, but the gambling bred antisocial behavior. Maybe I had it before. I never wanted to work for money. I wanted to find it the easy way. I turned to illegal maneuvers as early as 13. This has been my pattern up until the very recent present. I have had two years of high school.

I was in World War II. After the war I married a girl whom I knew for 42 hours; the marriage was annulled. Then in 1949, I remarried. I married a very steady girl with a child. A month after our marriage I got into legal trouble. I was gambling, by the way, at the time. It was my gambling money that paid for our wedding. I was sent away to prison for six years. I came out when I was 32, and we were divorced while I was away.

I went to work and I became acquainted with a young lady who worked there. We were friends for three years. During that three years my patterns of behavior hadn't changed. I gambled, I wheeled, I dealed. I resorted to anything and everything illegally to raise money for gambling, everything short of murder, which at times I contemplated. In 1960, my life was pretty twisted, I was going downhill. I didn't want to go back to prison, and I didn't know of GA. I couldn't get help from my family so I got married. I have to say honestly, I married for selfish reasons. I married for help. She was the complete opposite of me—highly moral, scheduled, kind, considerate. She got the worst of this bargain but idealistically, she thought my gambling would be under control as soon as we were married.

A year after we were married, push came to shove and she introduced me to GA. That was in 1961, nearly 18 years ago. I have been coming to GA for 18 years but not with a record of success. I have had many, many failures along the way. My longest period of abstinence was 22 months. I am not the typical story of a GA member who has been in for this amount of time. In fact, I am the enigma. During this time I think I have had only one serious job; certainly in the last 10 years I haven't had any serious work. I didn't deprive my family financially. I know that I deprived them emotionally. I always provided for them, and I gambled furiously. A couple of years ago I got in trouble again, and went back to prison for six months, all as a result of illegal maneuvers to have money for gambling. Before I went away I was attending GA meetings. I was very passive about the whole thing; I've been passive about it since day one. I truly didn't want to go to meetings. I would have preferred to stay home and watch T.V., but once I got there, I became involved. It penetrated. I listened. I helped a lot of people. At times, in the years I have been in, I participated in the group but more times than not I was a conscientious objector.

When I went away this last time, it hurt. It never hurt the first time, but it hurt this time. I missed everything. I swore that when I came out, no more. All the while I was away I never gambled once in prison. That was some kind of achievement. Gambling is part of the daily pastime. When I came out I looked for a new group. I wanted the strongest possible group. I knew I had to attend—not because the judge made it a condition of my probation—I had to attend because it is a way of life in my house because of my wife and her fierce devotion to Gam-Anon and its principles. I decided that I have to get the strongest group and get the most out of it and I did pick the strongest group. I have been out now just 13 months going to this group weekly, don't miss a single meeting, but I can't say that I haven't gambled in the 13 months, I have. I haven't gambled now in six months. But I have gambled a couple of times in spite of all the precautions I have taken. I have become a member of this group and it has been a great deterrent. If I didn't belong to this group, I may have gambled the entire 13 months. It is my participation with these people, socially as well as in meetings—my whole social life, by the way, consists of GA—that deters me. They are the only people we deal with.

For the first time in my 19 years of marriage I am in a position now where I am absolutely flat broke, no income. I had an income for the last year as a result of a business I had sold out when I went away, but even knowing all this time that my money was going to run out, I waited until the very last possible moment to go and seriously pursue a job, which I am doing now. This is indicative of how my mind works. The pie in the sky. Something is going to happen. Some deal will come along. Of course it hasn't. Now, in desperation I am reaching out for work. The thing that pleases me, particularly, in these last six months is that I haven't resorted to gambling. I haven't resorted to the means I used to use to gain money. Of course the reason for that is my constant reminder, my awareness, my being with people who at this stage of the game know, as I do, that compulsive gambling is a losing battle. I know I can't win gambling.

Now I know the answers and what has to be done and it took me all this time. Why am I so aware of it now? I am going through the same problem with one of my three children. He is an absolute carbon copy of me at his age, his attitudes, his answers. He is not into gambling but he is into other things that can do him no good. Over these last six months, because I have been concentrating, I see everything that he is doing and it hurts. It has completely taken me away from being wrapped up in myself. I am wrapped up in him. I am trying to deal with it. It is very difficult, the most difficult thing that I have ever had to deal with in my life. I've been involved with prison and courts, and bookmakers and shylocks, you name it, but this one is a tough one. I am handling it as well as I can because of my association with GA. I see my son's deficiencies and his problems and right now I am dedicated to trying to help him and let him possibly have the benefit of the things I had to suffer through. It is a difficult job.

I will close by saying I may not have reaped the full rewards of my association with GA, because there are people who have been in it as long as I have who have never gambled since the day they walked in. But I definitely know that I would be in far worse shape today, if I were here at all, if it weren't for my association with GA.

And, I'd like to add, although I originally got married for selfish reasons, my wife and I, through all these trying years, have come to love each other more and more. Her unfailing faith in me means more than I can ever say.

Gambler C:

I am a compulsive gambler. I must tell you it is a great honor to be a representative of GA, addressing this audience. As far as I can determine I was a compulsive gambler all my life. By the time I reached my early 20s, really nothing mattered except gambling, gambling, and more gambling. My compulsion for gambling was so intense that many times I would travel a couple of hundred miles, just to get "action." I was employed as a field auditor 12 years ago and remember vividly an assignment in Colorado. I would schedule my plans to see where there was action, because I had to have action. There was a dog track in Wyoming a couple of hundred miles away. I was on assignment for my company at that time for two weeks and every night I would travel 200 miles there and 200 miles back because I had to gamble. I had to have action. I'd bet on anything and everything. I could not be satisfied during the baseball season, for example, to bet just one game. I had to bet all 10 games, or 20 games, same thing for football. I had to play cards all the time.

The interesting thing is that I was a secret gambler. I was determined that my family would not know of my degeneration. I did a good job of it. I was a good manipulator. My bills were sent to my office. My wife wasn't attuned to financial matters, that was my responsibility. I did everything and anything to feed my habit. I extorted money from a crime syndicate at one time. It is quite possible I could have been killed but it didn't matter to me as long as there was a chance of getting money to feed my gambling habits. That was what was important.

Every day my energies would be spent either gambling or planning to gamble. First of all, I had to make sure I had enough money for gambling action that day. Second, there had to be time when I could read a racing program to handicap the horses. Then I spent the evenings getting results of baseball and football— quite often thinking of committing suicide at the end of the evening.

I was a real comedian. Either my wife wore blinders or I was one of the greatest actors who ever lived because she had no idea that she was married to this type of individual. I was a joker. I was well liked by everybody. I insisted upon paying the bills. I didn't deprive her of any of the necessities. I made sure bread was put on the table. This is the type of existence I led.

Six or seven years ago I thought psychiatric help might be it. The good doctor was able to tell me why I was gambling, but he wasn't able to stop my gambling. I have been in the program three years and fortunately I have been able to abstain in that period of time. I don't know why but I really don't care because, thank God, I am abstaining now.

I must tell you something that is very significant. As I have said, the only thing that mattered to me was gambling. I have to remind myself constantly, for my own sake, of the degenerate individual I was. I can give you a good example. My son is a brain-damaged child with emotional disorders to boot. He has been seeing doctors and going to special schools from the time he was two years old. He needs all the support that parents can give him. Many a time when I was gambling my wife would ask me to spend a little bit of time with my son to give him the companionship that he needed from a father. My way of living up to my responsibility would be to take him to an Off-Track Betting parlor. I wouldn't want him to go into an O.T.B. parlor because that would interfere with my functioning in handicapping the races. So I would lock him up in the car for two to three hours. The boy would be in a terrible sweat. God knows what permanent damage I caused that child. That is something I have to live with and that is something I have to constantly remind myself of. My compulsion is arrested. As far as I am concerned it is only arrested as long as I go to GA.

Now three years ago I hit rock bottom, not financially; there was still money to steal, to rob. I had been working for this company for 14 years but only went through the motions. I woke up one Sunday morning and I told my wife—bear in mind that I was a secret gambler—I told her all about it and I told her I owed in excess of $25,000, which is a lot of money for me. My wife is a very frugal individual; she worked hard for every penny she could save. She didn't come from a family that had any gambling habits. After taking some time to absorb this shock, she said, "If you told me you were a gigolo, a junkie, anything, I could tolerate that, I could understand that, but I just don't understand this." She didn't know if she wanted to live with me but she did insist upon one thing, she insisted that I call up GA.

I went to meetings and I have been going to meetings since then and I listen. It is very important to listen. It is very important for me not to become complacent. I know it is possible for me to gamble tomorrow and go back to my old habits. I listen and I give therapy and when I give therapy I talk about my gambling days. They are very painful. It is very painful to me when I talk about the harm that I did to my son, my wife, my family. It is very painful for me to realize that most of my life I was an insane individual, an irrational nonproductive individual. I have got to talk about those things when I give therapy because when I compare my life before I gambled to what has happened now it is just a miracle.

Dr. Custer talked about energy. I have a tremendous amount of energy, my energy was devoted to gambling. I am also getting ahead in the business world, and I always made a good living. I made a decent living before I gambled and in three years time the $25,000 has dissipated to almost nothing. I have been able to buy a house. My son goes to a special school. My income has almost doubled, and I feel that that is not the end of the potential I have in the business world.

Now anything is possible for me. I have the possibility of living up to that potential as long as I don't gamble. If I gamble I have no potential. I have to recognize that I will never be a social gambler because of my compulsiveness. I just can't gamble. What I have to do to stop gambling is go to GA meetings. That is the only thing that is good for me. As I said, I have to listen and I have to give good therapy. On my job I am out of town three, four days a week. I call up people, I give therapy on the phone. I see if there is a meeting in the town I am in. What I am really doing is getting my penicillin shot to arrest the disease I have. I am only on parole from hell. That is what it was. It was a living hell when I was gambling. GA for me is a life and death program. It is as simple as that.

Gambler A:

As I said before, I am a compulsive gambler—not only by everything that I know but everything that anyone else has ever been able to tell about me. When we were married for approximately eight years, my wife said she never knew that I gambled. Now I didn't gamble every day in the week. I didn't go to race tracks; I went to a track once in my life in Chicago. I went to one legalized gambling casino and that was in Cuba. I placed my five dollar bet and walked out with my wife on my arm, demonstrating that this meant absolutely nothing to me. I could take it or leave it. Once back in my home territory, where I grew up, where I went to school, where I worked, I gambled on everything possible. When I say everything, I mean that my response to almost every remark would be, "I bet you." If there was an argument it was, "I bet ya." I did not like race tracks too much because there were nine horses and nine jockeys and I thought all of them were crooked. It is easy to see that that was silliness. So, I went to the Indianapolis 500 and bet on how many people would die. I went to Kingsbridge Armory to bet on midget auto races. I went down to Madison Square Garden to bet on wrestling. I went any place, but without anybody else. I went by myself. I traveled to Ann Arbor, Michigan to watch a football game all by myself. For some reason or other I didn't enjoy, want, or need the company of other people when I was betting. I really didn't want anyone to know that I was betting. As I was growing up, my New Year's Eve consisted of driving down to Madison Square Garden to watch the

Rangers play the Bruins, all by myself. With 18,000 other nuts all playing with balloons and having a good time, I sat there watching the Rangers play the Bruins. By myself.

I have recollections of gambling as a kid—whether it was flipping baseball cards, pitching pennies against the wall, or playing strip poker, I played it with other kids. But one thing that was different from me and the others I realized later was that I was there first and stayed there longer. When the others would leave to go home for supper I'd still be there. I think that if I were born in Nome, Alaska, and never saw another individual and then suddenly dropped in the middle of New York City, I'd gamble, I'd bet. It would be compulsive.

I found that I took jobs, not for what they would pay me but for what I could get in side attractions in stealing. In the basement of my house is a little box; in that box are some baseballs, hard balls, and soft balls. When I was 13 years old I stole them from the people I worked for so I could sell them. I didn't buy candy, I didn't buy gum or toys. I just gambled with the money. If I bought the baseball cards that had gum in them it was only to get the baseball cards and I'd throw the gum away.

The only mark on my high school record is that I was caught pitching pennies. The principal knew I would not be in school on an opening day. She would come to me and say, what was the score, how was the game, whatever it was. I didn't have to bring notes from home. She knew. My parents didn't know. She knew. I then went on to college and I tried to pick a college that was far away from home, not because I didn't like my parents, but simply because it would give me, I thought, a freedom to do what I wanted to do; I could participate in gambling when I wanted to.

For four and a half years of college I did every form of gambling that I ever found—playing games like euchre, cribbage, poker, and bridge and whatever else that was there. I ran the football parlays at the university for three and a half years. You know what kind of money you can make at running football parlays at a college that has 20,000 students? In three and a half years I lost one bet. I worked full time at a book store. My parents sent me money, and I owed the housing unit where I lived when I left. I made more money illegally and legally when I was going to college than I earned the first five years I was married. But I had nothing. One day I paid my tuition for the next semester and I left, hoping that a change of environment back at home or doing some other work would help me to stop because I always knew that what I was doing was wrong. I shouldn't be gambling. I always knew that the people I associated with were not the people I should associate with and the places were not the places I should be. I liked none of it. I didn't like the people, the places, or anything connected with the gambling. I had no love of it whatsoever. I had no enjoyment, no fond memories, no recollections, nothing but pain. I was like a piece of the furniture. I neither smiled nor did I cry. I remember my parents said they stopped spanking me when I was about seven or eight years old because I would not cry. I would not laugh. I would not tell jokes. I was a loner. Me and my gambling.

The book store where I worked was across the street from a bank and I heard that John Dillinger had robbed that bank twice—once on the way down South and once on the way back up. I heard how much money he got from that bank and I laughed because I got much more than he ever got. My gun was a pen. I thought, you take from the rich not to give to the poor, you just take from the rich. The banks were the richest things I knew. So that is what I did. I took from the banks. All the way, any bank. In those days they didn't have your names on the checks. So right across from where I worked full time I would be cashing checks that didn't have my name on them.

All through my life people tried to help me—the dean, my parents, any employer I ever worked for, the bank president, psychiatrists, they all tried to help me. They all thought the best way to help me was to give me money. It would help me clear up my debts so I would have a clear mind to pay attention to what I was supposed to pay attention to. It didn't work out that way. It didn't work out that way at all. They weren't helping me. They were doing just the opposite, even though they meant well.

I spent much time, much money, much aggravation maybe, trying to find out why I gambled. I never found out why. I learned that it didn't make any difference why. I gambled. I fully accept the responsibility for everything I did. I cannot say that because I was sick or because something was wrong with me that I was not responsible for the acts I committed when I committed them, nor do I fail to accept responsibility for them now. I am responsible for me. I accept the fact that as a compulsive gambler, I cannot gamble again. If they come up with a pill, if they come up with an injection, if they come up with some serum, and say O.K., you take this and you will now be a controlled gambler, I don't want it! I don't want to gamble, either under control or out of control. Not interested. There are many other things that I have found in life that I do enjoy. If I did not enjoy gambling, why should I do something I don't like? What do I need it for? No longer. It helped me a lot that I was able to forgive myself. Oh, it took me so long to forgive myself! I was about six to eight months into GA, and some woman came up to me and said, "You know, I've known you six months now and I've never seen you smile." That is the way I was. A piece of furniture. I did not smile. I found that, when I gambled, it was like a nail being attracted to a magnet. I don't know why I did it. I don't know what got me there, but I went there.

I ended up my gambling by owning part of a crap game in a local town. Of course you can't have a gambling bit without payoffs. The whole bit, right? So I got involved in the illegal end of it, the payoffs, and for that I got called before a grand jury. In the middle of the grand jury room was the president of the bank where I had financed five cars that I didn't own, the bank where I conducted my personal and business banking. I stared at him for a long while and, finally, I guess I just said what I had to say. He thanked me for appearing, and he was the first person to really help me. He lifted me right off the ground. Later on I was able to go to him to borrow money in six figures in order to buy a business, to do things with my home. He just financed a car that I bought. I said, "Why do you lend me this money? You know what I am." You know what he said? "You paid us back, you didn't run away; you are staying with GA. Do you know how many people go bankrupt? How many people run away? You stayed here. You paid us back."

Well I paid them back and I paid a lot of other people back but after 17 years I am still paying back. It is not because I owed such a tremendous amount of money; it is because within our program, I was programmed so that I could meet my family obligations and the excess is used to pay off gambling debts. Even though I am now making more money, living in the same house, having the same number of cars, in the same business, I am still paying the same debts back the same way. I have not accelerated payment even though I could sit down and pay it off quickly. I realized a long time ago that this is to my benefit. It is going to help me the longer I pay back. The reminder is another thing that I need.

I forgot, as I was talking before, that I gambled in the stock market. Now, I did not *invest* in the stock market. I *gambled* in the stock market. I'd gotten the stockbroker's name from some papers of my grandfather, called him and introduced myself on the phone and said, "Would you be my stockbroker?" Now he could be sitting in the audience right now and I wouldn't know him if I fell over him. I then proceeded to call him up, to buy or sell. His commissions came to about $400 a month. I never saw a share of stock that I owned. It was too much trouble and too much money to send them back and forth. I knew how to read the ticker. I have had a subscription to the *Wall Street Journal* ever since I was 17 years of age. I was an economics major in college. I taught courses on the stock market in local high schools and I never lost a nickel on the stocks. But every nickel I made I would take and gamble somewhere else. I would take the buy and sell orders, the confirmations, to the poker table with me to show, even though I didn't have money. Look, I have it coming, I just sold the stock. Or, look, I just bought, I'll sell. I did not intend to pay people back that I borrowed money from. This was not my intent at all. Before coming to GA, I had no intention of paying anyone back. The only person who ever got money from me was someone who I could go to later on and get more money from—an increased amount, an additional amount. That is the only reason I would consider paying anyone back.

No one ever threatened me with jail. My wife never threatened me with divorce. No one ever threatened me with bodily harm and I dealt with people whom I had testified against, and not nice people, and that is being conservative. I did things I am not proud of and I constantly remind myself of those things simply because I feel that it will help me not to go back to doing them again. In GA, they say that repetition is not entertaining but it sure is educational. I constantly repeat to myself, this is what it was with me. I no longer can feel those persistent pangs of gambling. I have been removed from gambling for 17 years. I constantly remind myself of what I went through. Complacency is something I have to be constantly on guard against. I have not been without a GA meeting during this period of time for longer than 10 days. That is only because I went on vacation, which is something I never did before. I also never missed a day of work in 15 years. I couldn't. Too many notices came in the mail. Too many letters from banks. Too many bounced checks. Too many things that required me to scheme, dodge, and manipulate. I could not afford to take time off away from work. I had to be there. I had to be at that desk. I had to open the mail.

I own a business now. I am in the same business I was in when I came into GA. Most of us, as Dr. Custer pointed out, need two or more jobs to make it go. Obviously I couldn't make it go and, since I am a salesman, I contemplated taking another job. Then I said, now wait a minute, why don't I just work some more hours. So I started to work more hours. I get to the office at 8:15 in the morning and I leave the office about 7:15 at night, five days a week. And I work from 10:00 to 3:00 on Saturdays. So when you talk about a workaholic instead of a compulsive gambler, I guess that is what I have turned into. I am fortunate, I enjoy my work. Many people that I know are not that fortunate; they do not enjoy what they are doing. They do it to get the money.

So I have learned something else about myself. GA has not solved my problems; it has allowed me to see the problems and then to work on them. It took the blinders off. I was walking around with blinders on. I had problems, I have problems now. I never recognized any of the problems, and I didn't even attempt to try to solve them. Leave them alone, whatever it is will get better by itself. Leave it alone, don't talk about it. That is what I did. I started off betting with the money I would make in one hour on one bet. Then I would bet what I would make in one day. Then one week, one month. All of a sudden it was six months' salary on one bet. If I won the bet, who needs to go to work? If I lost it, the frustration! How can I gain all that back? I rationalized with myself, played games with myself. Why work? Even though I went to work every morning to get the mail, why work? I could never make enough money the way I looked at it to help me in gambling. It was an impossibility.

When I gambled, time meant nothing. I lost all sense of time, plus complete sense of money, plus complete sense of values. Time I am not going to get back. Money you make hand over fist but the thing that I am most happy about is I have gotten back a sense of values. When I was gambling, my wife said, "I want so and so." All right, get it. When the kids need this, go get it. I said to myself, I am gambling, spending all this money myself, this will keep them off my back. Not that I was that generous, just keep them off my back. Keep away from me! So, when I stopped gambling I had to learn how to say no because I couldn't afford those things and that was hard. It was a difficult thing for me to learn. I even had to learn how to say no without being abrupt and curt. How to say no without coming down with an axe. I went from the point of being the most dishonest person and the greatest liar to being honest and blunt.

I had such highs and such lows when I was gambling. I still have ups and downs but at least I am not way up and I am not way down any more. The group helps me tremendously. I have seen how other people can be happy and I have seen how other people have done the same things that I did, how they have worked together. "If you can do it, so can I" type of thing.

When I saw the psychiatrist and psychologist before coming to GA, I did not gamble. I thought it would be a complete waste of time, money, and energy to sit down with them and then gamble. So the entire time that I was involved with them I would not gamble. I said the same thing when I came to GA. I would not gamble as long as I came. So far, it has worked out well. It has been to my benefit. But these feelings that you get, they are hard sometimes to control. I remember watching a T.V. show showing a gambler making a lot of money in Vegas. The bottom line of it. I sat there in the middle of winter, in bed with one sheet on, no pajamas on, sweating, in a cramped position, watching this guy on this T.V. show go through the things that I had gone through. The bets and everything else and it was an experience. I was living through it. It was me there. About six months later it came up as a repeat on T.V. as everything does and my wife said, "Are you going to watch that?" I said, "No, I don't have to torture myself anymore. I saw it, that is it, and now I am finished. I don't have to regain something by watching the agony on someone else's face. The first time, fine, but not again."

I also learned through the group, I don't have to experience everything in life in order to know it is good or bad. I am now willing to take the experience of others. If Harry tells me the radiator is hot I don't have to go touch it to find out. I now believe it. I am a believer. I find that I have learned how to write checks, before I just wrote bad checks. In business I write a minimum of a hundred checks a month and they don't bounce. They don't bounce. People I am doing business with give me thousands of dollars of their money. If they can trust me, I now can trust me. I now have gained my self-respect, never mind respect of others. I now can walk down the street with my head up, I don't have to run to the other side of the street because someone I owe is walking towards me. I don't have to hide. I used to hide my car! You know what it is to hide your car? In a small town, too? When I played dice I didn't want anyone to know it and I had to hide the damn thing. I don't have to hide any more. I am on the ground floor and people know me. My name is in the book, I don't have an unlisted number and anyone who wants me can get a hold of me.

I have dealt with good people and bad people. I have dealt with people who come from all kinds of backgrounds and I'll tell you, I have learned how to live; before I was only existing. It is only a result of attending GA and going through a program like GA. I wasn't able to do it by myself because, as Sinatra sings, I did it my way. Well, I tried it my way for many, many years and my way, I learned, is not the good way and it is not going to help me. I am now willing to try someone else's way. I guess what we all say and what we feel is, we are the only game in town, GA. The only game in town. The only people who work with compulsive gamblers who have a desire to stop gambling. We don't charge anything. We don't want anything from the people, just their attendance.

It is people like you who can refer the people to us. It is people like you who spot compulsive gambling far faster than the spouse, far faster than the people who are close to the compulsive gambler. We have referrals from every type of mental health group, from doctors, from every place. And why we are here today is to say, hey, if you see people with a problem and they can't see it in themselves, don't want to admit it, or for some reason or another they can't admit it, we will help them. If they feel that their job will be in jeopardy, the home, whatever it is, they have the complete protection within our group. We are not going to reveal their names, their jobs, or anything else. Pretty soon they will feel just like I do now—it doesn't make any difference who knows what I am or what I did. *Now* is important.

Discussion

The gambling discussion was chaired by Robert Custer, M.D. Panel members were Rev. Msgr. Joseph A. Dunne, President and Executive Director, The National Council of Compulsive Gambling, Inc.; Leon D. Hankoff, M.D., Professor of Psychiatry, Department of Psychiatry and Behavioral Science, School of Medicine, State University of New York at Stony Brook; and the three members of Gamblers Anonymous.

Dr. Hankoff:

We have all agreed that there are people who get into terrible trouble because of gambling. We have not, however, agreed on the relationship of excessive gambling and the practice of medicine, relating to the more general theoretical issue of the relationship of disease to deviant behavior. Gambling is a universal piece of human behavior. It is often exercised to excess. When is it to be considered a disease?

In the scant medical literature on the subject, there is described the "compulsive gambler" distinguished by three features. First, the problem gambler is regarded as basically having a psychological rather than a social problem. The condition is chronic and often termed an "addiction."

Second, the "compulsive gambler" is described as an optimist who lives in a dream world with regard to his gambling. Third, he enjoys losing or in some way is driven to lose unconsciously.

Empirical studies find that there are a range of individuals who engage in excessive gambling for various motivations and with various personality patterns (Oldman, 1978). The number of individuals who could be considered chronic losers of the driven type is very small from among the large group of people who gamble or wager to some degree. Perhaps 2 to 3 percent of individuals seem to be patholocically involved in their gambling (Martinez & La Franchi, 1969). Apart from the pathologic aspects, this behavior we call gambling is worth viewing as a part of daily behavior seen in games of chance, sport, play, and even contests of skill. Anthropologic and sociologic literature gives us some insights into the subject of risk-taking behavior. Deliberate risk-taking behavior has survival value because it helps the individual to acquire the kind of equipment needed to deal with the unexpected.

Another anthropologic concept is one developed by an anthropologist named Victor Turner, but it has been broadly applied by others. That is the distinction between the structured state that we usually participate in—the 9:00 to 5:00, the family relationship, the structured world, as opposed to the transitional state, that kind of situation where the ordinary rules of life and relationships and directions are suspended while one goes through a transitional, relatively unstructured phase in which the rules are all different or at least all the daily rules are not operating. Now the non-structured phase is just as essential to total human adjustment as is the structured. Finally, the term used by J. Huizinga in his book *HomoLudens,* the ludic aspect of human functioning is another essential portion of man, unrelated to directed productive daily kinds of orderly performances. The ludic is the playful aspect, the imagined performance aspect of daily life, but representing a real human need.

I dwell on this because in it we can see an essential aspect of humanity that is the basis on which gambling is developed. Gambling builds on an essential human quality. Its excesses create the difficulties. If excessive gambling, pathologic gambling, is considered as evidence for a disease, what is the disease? Is the symptom of excess gambling, the disease? The other term used in relation to excessive gambling is "compulsive gambling." Does excessive or pathologic gambling qualify for the label of compulsive? Compulsion means, as Dr. Custer has mentioned, that the behavior is alien. If a behavior is ego-alien, the individual wants to resist it and, when carried out, it is accompanied by a negative feeling. A person is forced to do it against his will. The term "compulsive gambling," I think by and large, is not appropriate for the vast number of people who are pathologic gamblers. The behavior is not ego-alien, There is no truly compulsive quality about the gambling. To the contrary, the gambler's impulses are notoriously ego-syntonic. We have known for a long time that the gambler's enjoyment and involvement with his gambling is totally integrated into his personality. One observer, Charles Cotton, described it very well in 1674:

> Some say he was born with Cards in his hands, others that he will die so; but certainly it is all his life, and whether he sleeps or wakes he thinks of nothing else. He speaks the language of the Game he plays at, better than the language of his Country; and can less indure solecism in that than this...He loves Winter more than Summer, because it affords more Gamesters...He gives more willingly to the Butler than to the Poors-box, and is never more religious than when he prays he may win. He imagines he is at play when he is at Church; he takes his Prayer-book for a Pack of Cards, and thinks he is shuffling when he turns over the leaves...No man puts his brain to more use than he; for his life is a daily invention, and each meal a new strategem.

If the existence of a disease process is an explanation for excessive gambling as a symptom, it is circular reasoning to argue that the presence of the symptom proves the existence of a disease. The argument for a disease entity, such as compulsive gambling, is further complicated by the development of a treatment for the symptoms. The existence of a treatment may be taken as further evidence for a disease process. It should be clear that neither the presence of a presumed symptom nor a treatment form is proof of a disease process. As a disease entity in the strict medical sense, compulsive gambling is a rare syndrome to be found only in the psychoanalytic literature and at embezzlement trials. In labeling excessive gambling as compulsion or disease, an area of deviant behavior is medicalized and drawn into the field of treatment. With inadequate data we have formed a new diagnosis; with no data on treatment results we have developed a mode of treatment. Is there a justification for utilizing hospital beds and doctors' time in an already over-burdened and expensive medical care system for an unproven diagnosis and treatment of questionable effectiveness? On the other hand, nonmedical approaches such as those of Gamblers Anonymous appear to be a justified and sensible approach to this form of deviant social behavior.

My concerns with regard to designating compulsive gambling as a disease entity are three. The first is that in designating compulsive gambling as an illness, the afflicted individual is labeled as a patient and absolved of moral responsibility for his condition. Second, the patient is entitled to medical benefits and other compensations for his new-found illness. Third, the medical care system is stimulated to allocate treatment and resources for the disease.

On the other hand, the transition from gambler to patient status has a potential positive value. The gambler who accepts an illness label for his actions may have achieved an important first step in viewing his behavior as aberrant. In other words, I am quite willing to accept the gambler's definition of himself as a diseased or sick person, if it is his way of asking for help. It may represent a considerable degree of insight on the part of the gambler over previously noncritical attitude toward his behavior. To this extent the illness label, artificial as it may be, may serve a useful practical function, just as it does for some alcoholics, representing the first small step in the direction of increased self-awareness. The gambler in treatment, even as a means of avoiding blame, has thus accepted a status as a patient, moving away from total denial. Medical treatment thus can begin the process of moving the individual from no awareness of his deviance to a sense of responsibility for his treatment.

In sum, while excessive or pathologic gambling is a fairly common phenomenon, a specific entity of truly ego-alien compulsive gambling is probably extremely rare. Symptomatic gambling, as a feature of other psychiatric conditions is one subgroup of pathologic gambling, for example, the manic-depressive patient in the manic phase who gambles away his money. Finally the behavioral and emotional problems may arise consequent to or secondary to excessive gambling. These require psychiatric treatment or other forms of assistance, but themselves do not represent a specific gambling illness.

Let me finish with my recommendations since I have questioned the placing of gambling in the illness arena despite the DSM-III diagnosis which I think will be largely misapplied. My solution is twofold. One, when the psychiatrist is involved in the management of deviant behavior as opposed to defect or disease, the psychiatrist functions only as an adjunct or ancillary person in the picture, without primary responsibility. The psychiatrist may contribute as a consultant or even treat secondary symptoms, but he is not the essential caregiver in terms of management. The second point I would make about the involvement of psychiatry in the management of the deviant behavior called "excessive gambling" is that the crux of the mismanagement in psychiatry and psycho-therapy in relation to gambling and other forms of deviant behavior is the issue of value systems. Gamblers Anonymous, I believe, confronts the individual, the citizen (in GA the gambler is not a patient obviously) with a value system and makes no bones about it. The gambler is invited to view his missteps, his abuse of other people, and to do something about it and to make full restitution. By and large, in the field of psychiatry, particularly those parts of it that are involved in psychotherapy, we muddle along, claiming to be nonjudgmental and claiming to eschew value judgments. This is absurd. There is no value-free activity on the part of a human being. What I am suggesting as a solution to this issue is that the psychiatrist or psychotherapist make this very clear in terms of his relationship to a prevailing and significant value system in working with the issue of deviant behavior.

Dr. Custer:

I tend to agree with most of what you say. At our particular stage of knowledge, we are so early into this problem that I think we will find out much more about the problem as there are so many unknowns.

But I suspect that many things that you say may be wrong. I was recently in court testifying about compulsive gambling. This particular individual had embezzled about $140,000 and was to go to prison for 15 years. He was a very capable attorney who, of course, was going to lose the bar but he would be able to make money in many ways. I suggested to the judge what I felt was necessary, that he stop gambling, get treatment with Gamblers Anonymous and with the Veterans Administration, and make full restitution of all the money he had taken. Now that doesn't sound too much like a bailout to me. What sounds like a bailout to me is that he would go to prison on a 15-year charge, be out in three years, and would not owe a cent. He would then resume his gambling career at that point.

I think, particularly in treatment, we have to deal with the reality of not using a therapist as a bailout; that is one of the things I am very much opposed to. We can't keep going with the same processes that the family had done, the friends had done, the in-laws had done, to continue the problem. I think it is a real danger that the professionals would get involved that way. Our program has been strictly the opposite. I remember when the judge told this particular defendant that he had a choice, he could go to prison or he could stay out and make restitution and get treatment, there was a moment of hesitation on his part as to which he was going to choose. The judge reminded him at one point that if he found out that he was gambling after he had been on probation for 14 years and eight months, he could bet a dime he would send him back to prison for 15 years. That doesn't sound to me like a bailout.

My background is in alcoholism, so this is sort of like *déjà vu*. I went through the same thing more than 20 years ago, because alcoholism wasn't called a disease, and I wasn't concerned about what it was called when I was a young physician. All I knew was that I had patients on my hands who had DT's and there was no way I could get them into the hospital. They would not accept them. I detoxified DT's left and right at home, which was fairly adequate if you have a lot of people and a lot of stamina, but at the same time that is no way to deal with that type of problem.

I think the introduction of the disease concept has made it easier to treat some of the physical and psychological aspects, and I think we have made headway. I would be perfectly happy for AA to do all the detoxification and to deal with the problem and I think they probably could. But I don't think they were getting much support either; they did not get much support until the A.M.A. recognized that it was an illness. There was a significant jump in the number of people who were treated in AA after alcoholism became recognized as an illness. I don't know that I am particularly happy about it being recognized as an illness; I am just particularly happy about an awful lot of alcoholics getting treatment. I certainly am not opposed to risk-taking behavior. I think it is very valuable not only for our survival but for enriching our lives. When we are talking about gambling, I am in no way opposed to legalized gambling, and I don't think the problem is gambling. I think that the problem is the gambler. I am not even opposed to the recommendations of how we might deal with it. One of the things that came out in the recommendations that I was happy to hear was that the psychiatrists should function in an ancillary way. I don't think psychiatrists do very well in some of these areas, but they can give a lot of support to Gamblers Anonymous. The fact that they are accepting of the compulsive gambler in treatment, that they are accepting of Gamblers Anonymous, that they know about them, that they will refer to them, is invaluable in moving the compulsive gambler towards changing his behavior whether it is deviant, disease, addicted, or whatever.

In the Cleveland area, when we first explored the possibilities of starting an inpatient unit, we checked with GA in the area and found their retention rate was less than 5 percent. Since the program has been introduced in the Cleveland area, we have worked very closely with that group—they meet at the hospital, they bring the patients to the hospital, three nights a week they take them to other meetings. The retention rate now in GA for the ones going through that program is almost 60 percent. We don't necessarily have an opportunity to follow them. We have to refer them out for their follow-up with Gamblers Anonymous groups and they do very well. So I think that sometimes it is very helpful to get the treatment started, get them organized, get their head on straight, give them a direction, and then refer them to a very effective group such as Gamblers Anonymous. The single most effective treatment for compulsive gamblers is Gamblers Anonymous.

Rev. Dunne:

I have been associated now with Gamblers Anonymous as a friend, as a rabbi, for possibly 20 years. At their request we established the National Council on Compulsive Gambling; this is very similar to the National Council on Alcoholism.

Our function is to educate, make aware, broaden the knowledge of every spectrum of our society—the medical profession, the criminal justice system, the educators, the community, and so forth. We have dedicated ourselves to this. Our motivation is to make people aware of compulsive gambling as an illness.

We do not accept the statement that compulsive gambling is a minor illness. We know from long, sad experience that all the surveys, particularly the one conducted by the Commission on Review of National Policy Toward Gambling, do not present the real picture in our country. People in Gamblers Anonymous know better than anybody else the extent of this illness.

When the figures come up from a limited sample of 1,746 people across our country, that there are 1.2 million compulsive gamblers in the country, we know that that is not right, it is wrong. All you have to do is look in an O.T.B. parlor as you are going by, or possibly go into an O.T.B. parlor. Go to Roosevelt Raceway on the coldest night in the year, or see the people at Aqueduct in the afternoon waiting for the bus to Roosevelt that night, or deal with what we deal with—the people, the families, the children of compulsive gamblers, and you will know that it is not a minor illness. It is not restricted to 3 percent. It is much bigger. It is all over the country and in every phase of our business life.

We programmed the outgoing calls from a large insurance company in New York City and found that more than half the phone calls going out of that company were to O.T.B. during business hours. Almost every time you find a vice-president of a bank involved in embezzlement, you know there is gambling involved. Being in the police department, I should know a little bit about organized crime. The robbery at Lufthansa Airways was a direct result of the fact that employees owed a great amount of money and, in order to get off the hook, they gave the plans necessary to rob that establishment. So it is not a minor problem.

I know doctors who are compulsive gamblers. They perform very expensive operations in the morning, but there is a car waiting at the hospital to take them to the track that afternoon. I know clergy who are compulsive gamblers. It is in all phases of our life. I know complete unions; I know complete industries that are being bankrupted by compulsive gamblers. I know one large company whose very existence was almost destroyed by a comptroller who was a compulsive gambler. So it is not a small problem.

We see in Gamblers Anonymous the lucky people who, through the grace of God and a brave wife who made a phone call, were able to find help. We have doubled the number of GA meetings in New York City since O.T.B. We have now found at least three new meetings in South Jersey since Atlantic City opened gambling casinos. So it is a huge problem.

Second, I resent the attitude on the part of the medical profession, denying sick people the benefits of their insurance policies. I have two sergeants in the police department who as veterans were sent to Brecksville and who are today productive people, because they availed themselves of the right to this kind of treatment. I think every compulsive gambler has as much right to treatment for compulsive gambling as he has for alcoholism and drug addition. This is a democracy, and it is our purpose in the Council to educate people so they are aware of this illness.

As Dr. Custer said, in the beginning alcoholics were rejected by most professions, including the clergy. Statistics show that many alcoholics made their first inquiry for help to the clergy and didn't get much help. But, we got less help from other professions. We understand the human qualities, we understand the lack of education in medical schools, we understand the inconvenience and the problems about handling certain people in the community, but I think that the day will come when all our sick people will have a right to treatment.

Thanks to Dr. Custer's example, and as result of the work of the Council, we hope that soon we will get treatment for these people who are dying, who are committing suicide. We have a boy up for a 15-year sentence for selling cocaine and no one in the court asked, why was this boy selling cocaine? The judge didn't ask, the district attorney didn't ask, even his own legal counsel didn't ask, until the parents told us he was selling cocaine to support his gambling habit. Now, thank God, we are getting cooperation from the courts and we are getting people into treatment. That is only the beginning. We need your help. You are here because you are interested in compulsive gambling as a treatable illness. There is help for these people and we hope that more people in the medical profession take an interest and assist us in this important work.

Gambler A:

Whether it is an illness or not an illness or a sickness or not a sickness, I don't care what you are going to call it—people need help. We have people, not statistics. I don't care what the percentages are. I don't care whether it is an illness. I don't care how you look at it. It is a problem. It is an invisible problem, and therein lies the basis of our biggest difficulty. People cannot recognize that this problem exists in someone else. The trained people, like you are, cannot recognize that when someone comes with a marital problem, with an absentee problem, with a financial problem, with any of these other problems, that the basis of this problem is compulsive gambling. Whether or not the insurance companies are paying for the confinement, really I couldn't care less.

Give us the facilities, the people and the manpower and you refer people, and ask the question, dig into it, find out.

Audience:

One of the things I was fascinated by in the discussion by the three people from GA was that they talked about keeping their activities secret. I've seen only a few pathologic gamblers in my practice. None of them came to me with that as the primary complaint. They came with other complaints, and it came out that they were pathologic gamblers. What I found out in each case was that the introduction of these people to gambling as a regular part of their lives was done by their families, by their parents. In no instance did the patient tell me this. In each instance I had the opportunity to speak to the parents and the parents just casually revealed it. In each case, it was a question of the track. The parent took them to the track, the parent gambled, and let the kid gamble. The interesting thing was the boys were brought by mama and the one girl I saw was brought by papa. I am wondering if this is something that is a regular thing for pathologic gamblers.

Gambler C:

I think I mentioned that I categorize myself as a secret gambler. My uncle was a compulsive gambler and I would classify my parents as social gamblers. When I started maturing in the program and abstained from gambling, I concentrated not on whose fault it was—and it would have been easy to blame parents and uncles and people who had, perhaps, a gambling problem—I concentrated on the fact that this is my problem and I had to resolve it. My brother wasn't affected by it. I have seen other people whose parents were compulsive gamblers not affected by it. I happened to be affected by it. I couldn't begin to recover by starting to blame them. I have to resolve my own problems. I can't dwell on whose fault it was. As far as I was concerned, it was my fault. I had to work it out and I worked it out with GA.

Gambler B:

In answer to that question, I am a product of a home with compulsive gambling. I told you I came from a split home. I was brought up by my mother, and my mother was a compulsive gambler. I started gambling at 13, because I was taking her bets to the corner candy store. That was my introduction. And it took me a long, long time to realize that my mother's moral standards were not quite that of the norm. She condoned the gambling and she even condoned my stealing to supplement my gambling. So I had a tough uphill battle right from the beginning and, with no help until 1961, my pattern was pretty well set. Gambling and stealing became a way of life.

Audience:

Is the recovering gambler able to handle monies, to make investments, or to provide financial security? Does he have to abstain from that?

Gambler A:

We would advise the compulsive gambler not to handle money. Almost categorically. We know people who own businesses who want to invest the money of the pension fund and we try and force them to get someone else to control the investments.

Audience:

Dr. Custer, could you please describe the details, as briefly as possible, as to what constitutes the program at Brecksville so that we are all talking about the same thing.

Dr. Custer:

Let me give you one little important piece of history before I go into that. We were approached by three members of Gamblers Anonymous and they asked, do you think you might be able to help us? They had been coming to AA meetings and I would lecture there and they thought maybe they would be able to help and we discussed this with the staff. The staff was enthused about the idea. So we started going to GA meetings and Gam-Anon meetings, getting through the literature which took a very short time. We decided then that if we were going to bring in a group that was listed as having a problem (we were a little skeptical as to whether it really existed), then let's go ahead and record everything, all the psychological data, cultural data, physical data, and anything we could get. We also wanted to record a lot of observations. We were fortunate we had a trained staff because they were running the alcoholism unit at that time. So what we did when we first brought them in was to start recording everything. It was sort of intensive as it started out, doing the physical exams, getting all the testing. Somewhere within that first day or so they just seemed to be wired for some sort of electricity, you almost couldn't get close to them. That is when we began to hear about the diarrhea, and the abdominal pain, and the cold sweats, and they were stammering. We thought for sure they were also drug abusers and alcoholics, which we tested out and found that indeed they weren't, and checked with the families and indeed they weren't. We started then to use different medications to see if we might bring this down and the medications were just generally ineffective.

We had a very active physical therapy program; we used to play basketball and swim, things of that nature, and they got into that and enjoyed it. But, with what ventilation we could get from them at that time, they were pretty hostile. What we did initially in that treatment program was to just try to get them to tell their story and get them talking and that seemed to bring them down some, too. They were very eager to walk out the door and start gambling again and the door was always open; they could go out at any time. I think I mentioned that only two out of the first 100 walked out the door before the treatment was completed.

Most gamblers get together as a group and help out very much with the detoxification of the alcoholics and they are involved in patient government. So it is that amount of activity that was another thing that we found was very valuable and we capitalized on it. The gamblers invariably became presidents of the patient governments. They ran things. They ran the most elaborate recreational programs we ever had. They still hold all the records for winning the bowling tournaments and for the highest scores we have ever had. They were real promoters. They helped out within their wards and their help overflowed to other parts of the hospital. I remember one time, I was chief of staff, when one of them volunteered to do all my work for me. I felt badly because I felt he could probably do it better.

We get into group therapy very actively. It is a very lively type of thing. We deal with feelings and there are a lot of confrontations going on. There is individual therapy depending upon special problems, and we also tie in with the families. We have Gamblers Anonymous, which meets in the hospital. Of course we also have lectures and didactics.

The program is intensive. It isn't that we are trying to make it intensive; they make it intensive.

Audience:

The gentlemen from Gamblers Anonymous are very articulate and express themselves very well. Does assertiveness training play a part in this?

Dr. Custer:

I am sure Mr. A wasn't this assertive 16 years ago. When he would be faced with a problem, he would back off from it. If his wife challenged him, he would sulk, and would have a good reason for going ahead and gambling. I am sure it was that type pattern. His assertiveness has developed because of his treatment program, I'm pretty sure.

If we took profiles of the ones who came through, I would say that one of the largest groups are the passive-aggressives. I think that passive-aggressives do very well in assertiveness training.

Gambler C:

When I first joined Gamblers Anonymous, my self-esteem was below zero. When I walked into a room I thought I was the only person in the world who had this illness. Then I met people from all walks of life. I met cab drivers, I met corporate vice-presidents. I met successful people who had a high degree of intelligence. All this certainly helped my recovery and my assertiveness.

Audience:

What about withdrawal symptoms? When do they occur? How long do they last?

Dr. Custer:

If a person had sworn off gambling for several weeks or so, and then came in, we didn't see these symptoms. But when they came in and said, I just have to stop, I am in terrible shape, I must stop, I want treatment, I just gambled this day; those were the ones who usually within about 24 hours would start off by literally having tremors, headaches, cold sweats. Stammering was very common, as were gastrointestinal symptoms, diarrhea, vomiting, and nausea. They were very restless, they didn't sleep, complained about nightmares, were up frequently during the night. It surprised us and we were not quite sure what it was. After this occurred several times, I asked one of them, "Well, what do you think might help this?" He said, "I know what would help me. If I could just go out and gamble, all these symptoms would go away. I've had this before." This is when I got the first clue that maybe this was a type of withdrawal. Then, exploring it with the others, it seemed to be a fact that they might even develop symptoms like this on a Sunday when no gambling was available. They were restless and paced like tigers.

Audience:
Did you use any major tranquilizers?

Dr. Custer:
No, I didn't, but I think that is a very good point. What we found was that getting them into that quick routine and really drilling them in a sense to burn it out, seemed to work well, plus the fact that we always had somebody available to talk to them. I saw more and more as we started getting sleep histories, that they really hadn't been getting very much sleep for quite a period of time—say from 5 to 10 days. I really felt that they were not getting much more than two or three hours sleep. This is a type of thing we frequently saw in our soldiers when they were in combat situations and had very little sleep. I would sure like to study it more.

Dr. Hankoff:
The question of withdrawal gets us back to the matter of disease, illness, medicalization of pathologic gambling. I am reminded of the line in "The Hunting of the Snark," Lewis Carroll's poem where the person says: "There I have said it three times and what I have said three times is true." But I suppose we can haggle and call it anything we want and there isn't much point to debating it if what we have said three times is true. The point I have been trying to make is this: that having declared something a medical illness in the strict medical sense, you have altered the value system, the form of judgment of the behavior, and you have absolved the individual of personal responsibility. This is the logical error

that we make. Most of the time when we say that we are dealing with an illness, we assume then the behavior comes from cell, or hormone, or endocrine substance, or what-have-you, and therefore somehow the individual does not have to be concerned about personal responsibility. Gamblers Anonymous emphasizes the contrary and I am concerned that we will dilute their efforts by saying it three times.

I will give two other examples. One is that all three individuals who spoke today about their experiences told of the failure of conventional psychiatric, i.e. medical, treatment, as well as of psychotherapy by nonmedical therapists. The other example is this, there was once a condition called homosexuality. A few years ago it was a crime, then it became an illness, and now we don't know what it is. The point is that in all of these confusing situations, it does not pay to say it three times, to give it a name, and then decide that we have solved the logical problems involved.

Dr. Custer:

I have to agree with Leon on that. I don't want to say it a fourth time. I was just as skeptical as Leon is at one time, but I think it is very important to look at this problem, to study it, and do more research on it. Why fuss about the diagnosis? I don't think it is quite right when you say that Gamblers Anonymous does not talk about this as an illness; they say the individual must assume the responsibility but simultaneously they say it is an illness.

Dr. Hankoff:

Gamblers Anonymous can call it an illness; it is when a physician calls it an illness that we are in trouble.

Dr. Custer:

What are we really in trouble with?

Dr. Hankoff:

We are in trouble in that we have medicalized it, and it is a self-serving act that we have gone through because we are making patients for ourselves. Every time the industry of psychotherapy enlarges its domain it adds patients and more possibilities for getting involved with more areas of deviance and more, of course, unsuccessful and expensive kinds of excursions into the area treatment of unproven treatments.

Dr. Custer:

Now we have both said it three times.

Rev. Dunne:

I believe that all of us, as Dr. Custer said, must study, must make ourselves available to give these people whatever help we can give them. Whether we diagnose it as an illness, as a personality disorder, or just deviant behavior, we have no right to deny them the help that is due them.

Audience:

Is legalized gambling detrimental to the compulsive gambler?

Gambler A:

Gamblers Anonymous takes no position whatsoever.

Rev. Dunne:

On the other hand, the National Council does have something to say. All our studies indicate throughout the country that the primary problem with gambling and the increase of compulsive gambling is due to accessibility. If people are not close to gambling there is a much less degree of addiction. The highest degree of addiction to compulsive gambling is in Las Vegas. They have three times the incidence of compulsive gambling than does any other place in the nation.

The Council itself does not take a position for or against legalization but we certainly believe in educating communities to understand the impact of gambling, to look at it in its true perspective. Number one, the legalization of gambling does increase the number of compulsive gamblers. That has been proved by off-track betting. Second, the monies realized from various types of gambling, particularly casino gambling, are not really worth the effort to the state. They cannot realize the great amounts of money they promise or they expect. Third, it does not take money away from organized crime. If anything, it contributes to the take of illegal gambling because more people are exposed to gambling, and then by moving ahead in their gambling habits they find out that O.T.B. and legalized gambling do not give credit, but there is a man outside the store who gives credit, the bookmaker. When they get further indebted to him, he steers them to a shylock who lends them money to gamble. Now they are involved in real serious trouble.

I would say that citizens should think long and hard before they vote for any type of legal gambling. Study it very carefully. In all the communities we have addressed, they have voted it down once they know the full impact of legalizing gambling. The "big win" is a panacea that is never realized and our country is going through another long period of suffering. In the Colonies there were lotteries to support public projects, but before the Civil War, every lottery was legislated out of existence by the federal government because of corruption. There is something very corruptive about gambling and people should know and weigh these things and then vote according to their own minds.

Audience:

Have there been any animal lab studies done that would compare to the gambling behavior in human beings?

Dr. Custer:

Yes, B.F. Skinner has done many behavioral studies with rats. He found that a schedule of reinforcement in which there was random intermittent reinforcement was much more effective than a fixed-ratio schedule. When reinforcement is given on a random basis—as is the case with gambling—the rat's behavior is very difficult to extinguish. I think one of the most interesting studies was one that Richter came up with at Johns Hopkins. It is not related to gambling but I tend to relate it to gambling. He decided to see how his laboratory rats would do as far as swimming is concerned, how they could survive. So he put them in a tank and most of them drowned in about two hours. Then he said, what I would like to do is go down to the waterfront here in Baltimore and get the real survivors, the big rats, and see how they compare with the pantywaists I have here. So he got some of those rats, put them in water, and those rats drowned in about two minutes. Richter, being very bright and alert, said, what I think I will try is just before they drown I will bail them out. He did that. Then, when he put them back in the water, they swam for 96 hours. It is sort of symbolic, and may reflect on the danger of bailout for compulsive gamblers. Once they get that bailout they are off and running.

Gambler C:

You mentioned a reward. When I was gambling, I stole, I cheated, I robbed, I extorted money, I was nonfunctional in society. I didn't communicate with my family, I couldn't care less about that. Just to get my high—that was the most positive thing. I got a tremendous high from gambling and if I went back to gambling tomorrow, and I speak only for myself, I would get a tremendous high. Now you talk about the reward. If you abstain from gambling the rewards are living up to whatever potential you have, being a member of society—something that maybe the people in the audience take for granted—a little self-respect. For the first time in my life since I have abstained from gambling I have self-respect. I can look at myself in the mirror and not be ashamed of what I see. I am successful in the business world. So we have a reward system of our own and we recognize it and it is very meaningful.

Audience:

Regarding the relationship between compulsive gambling and the proliferation of O.T.B. and legalized gambling, it seems to me that the compulsive gambler will find action regardless of whether it is accessible or not. As Mr. C mentioned this morning he traveled 200 miles for action. So it seems to me that legalized gambling doesn't make the compulsive gambler more compulsive, it just makes gambling more accessible.

Rev. Dunne:

Your argument is presuming that he is compulsive to start with. My explanation is that people, seeing a betting shop, go in and experiment and, little by little, they become addicted and compulsive. The more shops you have the more people are going to experiment and the more are going to be addicted. New York State is not pushing the sale of alcohol. New York State licenses the sale of alcohol; but the State of New York is pushing gambling. Therefore the position of the Council is that we will support no legislation regarding legalization of gambling unless the state also agrees to supply treatment for the victims of public policy.

Audience:

My question has to do with the people who have more to gain than the individuals who are being treated. I am talking about business in general. Business probably has more to gain by treating and helping sick people than anyone else. We are talking about the dollars that are lost in industry as a result of absenteeism, nonperformance, and so forth. How does business itself respond to the search, the literature, the information that these organizations can provide?

Rev. Dunne:

It is a difficult uphill battle, just as it was in the field of alcoholism, to convince an employer, a personnel director, or a president of a company that the company is losing countless hours because of gambling on the part of the employees.

I have here a list of things to look for if you are an employer. The first thing to watch for is appearance of nonemployees on the premises. People are picking up bets, making payoffs, and distributing racing forms. The lengthy use of the pay telephone at the same time each day, especially before 1:30 when the Daily Double closes. Calls from wives complaining that the workers are not bringing home the paychecks. Why? Because they are being collected right after payday by bookmakers or shylocks. Paychecks of several employees are endorsed over to the same person, maybe a bookie or a loan shark. We had a case yesterday of a person stealing his friend's paycheck and cashing it. Evidence of gambling is found in a plant by betting pools and slips. Increasing attempts to obtain wages of employees. People putting claims on their pay. Regular visits to all the departments by an employee whose job does not require moving about the plant; he is picking up bets. Many employees drift to a central location in the plant at certain times of the day. Salary advances regularly requested. Those are many earmarks that gambling is going on in the plant. We try to persuade companies to educate their personnel people to ask, to inquire whether or not a problem is related to gambling. The insurance industry has published a booklet to acquaint insurance companies with the problem. They are really paying the tab for most of the losses. So industry today is taking a hard look at it. There is a large organization called the Economic Development Council of the City of New York that prepares studies and policies for the city. They are looking at gambling very carefully. We are trying to help all these people to ferret out the compulsive gamblers and give them an opportunity to recover.

Audience:

I would like to know how often you find cross addiction of gambling and drug or alcohol abuse. How do you decide what the primary disorder is? It would seem logical to get the mind clear first of the alcohol or the drugs.

Dr. Custer:

With the first 100 who went through our program, 6 percent were involved with drugs—mostly the softer drugs, marijuana, some barbiturates—and 4 percent with alcohol, for a total of 10 percent with both problems. We didn't have too much of a problem with the drug usage because it was coming in later, the gambling had already started. It helped a little to know which one preceded.

I think, generally speaking, with the ones we did have, certainly the compulsive gambling dominated in the drug issue. With the alcoholics, it did become a problem. We had to detoxify them and then try and work that out. It gets very difficult to say whether they start off drinking and then with that loss of judgment end up gambling foolishly. I think if we dissect back through the history, we find them using both and it is very difficult to separate them.

One of the things we did find was as they stopped their gambling behavior, they were much more vulnerable to increasing the amount of alcohol. We dealt with that pretty regularly in the inpatient program to make sure that didn't happen because alcohol was a substitute they could fall back on. There are different reports as far as the incidence of both alcoholism and compulsive gambling; or do compulsive gamblers drink more anyhow? Though there are differences of opinion, and I am sure there are right here, what I found is the compulsive gambler tends not to drink much at all while he is gambling. Once the gambling stops then he might use the drinking to sort of help him get to sleep or unwind. He uses it as a sleeping medication frequently. With the alcoholic who gambles, that becomes a dangerous and explosive type of thing in which they can lose money very quickly. I don't think we have answered that question on the basis of the statistics we do have.

Gambler A:

We found we can't deal with the dual problem with only one of the programs—in other words, the alcoholic who gambles or the gambler who is alcoholic. Alcoholics Anonymous cannot handle the gambling problem of the alcoholic and Gamblers Anonymous cannot handle the alcoholic problem of the gambler. I don't understand this because both programs are basically the same, but we have not been able to handle one case that I know of. Not one! So we refer to each other. We send the alcoholic gambler to AA and they send the gambling alcoholic to us.

Gambler B:

I'd like to comment on gambling and the crossover with alcohol and drugs. I am a compulsive person. I use alcohol, I use marijuana, and I gamble. I can control the alcohol, it has never caused me a problem. I can control the marijuana, it has never caused me a problem. I can't control the gambling. I have absolutely no control over it. None.

I would like to illustrate to you how I have no control over it, and I am not a stupid person. In 1977, I was arrested in three states for three different illegal activities all relating to gambling. The first one I got a probation. For the second one in Virginia I pleaded not guilty in front of a judge and he continued the case to another time. I had to be in New York the next morning so I drove from Virginia to New York and I think that a normal person would have known what he was facing, what he had to go through, what he had to contend with. I only had one thing on my mind because I was in action. I drove from the lower part of Virginia as fast as that car could go because I knew I had to pass Bowie Racetrack on the way up to be sentenced. I half killed myself to get there for two lousy races that made no difference. The amount of money I would have won or lost I don't think would have been that significant to my future. But I felt so good getting there. Then I was able to drive comfortably the rest of the way to New York.

The next morning I was sentenced to prison. I asked for 30 days to get my affairs in order. My affairs in order! I had some things to attend to. That night, the next day, I was in action, I was gambling. After he sentenced me I went on with my gambling spree. Then my friends in GA whom I had known for all these years found out and they wanted to help me. They didn't feel that imprisonment would solve the situation and they suggested I go to Brecksville to try to get help. The judge reconsidered and I was sent to Brecksville.

I went there with an open mind. I got there on a Monday and I had gambled the day before, on Sunday. For 10 days I listened. I didn't participate fully, but I didn't try to con anybody. In the back of my mind I was hopeful that the judge would take this into consideration and possibly alleviate my sentence. But on the eleventh day a strange thing happened.

We had been participating in therapy on a daily basis, and I did a lot of listening. I didn't do too much talking. For 10 days we had done nothing but concentrate on one subject, compulsive gambling. No wife, no kids, no gambling, no nothing. In all due respect, Dr. Custer, it was pretty much like prison. We weren't allowed off the grounds and on the eleventh day some guy was talking who had just come in from Vegas. He was in bad shape. He was a verbal mess. I wasn't. I don't even remember what he was saying. I made some comments and he said something to me, and I don't know, the thing I've been waiting for all my life, happened. I just broke down. I didn't have one single defense left, and I let it out. I let it out that I knew how sick I was. I knew what I was doing, I knew what I needed, and it came out of me and I broke down afterwards. I cried. I just didn't know which end was up but I never felt so good in my life because it was the first time that I ever penetrated. The first time that I really believed in what I was saying and doing.

Audience:

Withdrawal symptoms seem to be physiologic. I have heard gamblers talk about something called a "rush." They said that when they won big they got a euphoric feeling, almost like dizziness. It was like getting high. Is it possible that there are physiologic effects?

Dr. Custer:

I often wonder whether we haven't been looking at the whole problem of abuse in the wrong way. I think we have been looking at the substances and I think that has blurred our vision. I think maybe if we looked a little more at the psychological part of it, we might have better understanding. We are very interested in detoxification and abstinence and possibly we spend too much time with that and don't deal with their life style and how they adjust and cope with life. I think when you see compulsive gamblers over a period of time, either in or out of action, I have the feeling they are in a fantasy world because I can be very close to them or say hello to them and they don't see me, depending on how things are going with the gambling. I don't really know what is going on physiologically with them. Maybe this is part of what they already have or is the gambling itself producing it?

Audience:

Have there been any studies?

Dr. Custer:

No. One thing that I would really find interesting to do, and I suspect it might be very effective for a subgroup of compulsive gamblers, is to see how they do on lithium. Yet, there is not one dollar in this country for research funds on compulsive gambling. We don't have a cent to try anything at this point.

Audience:
Do you do any enzyme profiles on the inpatients?

Dr. Custer:
Yes, we have. We haven't found anything remarkable.

Audience:
What kind of criteria do you have for accepting someone at Brecksville? Do you have to determine motivation like we have to do in alcoholism?

Dr. Custer:
No. When we started the program the only criteria for acceptance was that first they had to be eligible veterans. So we get only veterans. But second, we accept anybody who wants to come in for treatment. We did that intentionally because we had to find out what group we are going to get. This was very helpful because out of that first 100 compulsive gamblers, we saw seven classic antisocial personalities whose gambling was a part of their lives and all they were in for was a boat ride. We did not kick those people out; we wanted to study them as well so that we could differentiate them from the compulsive gambler. I think that has helped considerably. Incidentally, we weren't able to help that group at all. I am sure some other program could, perhaps even Gamblers Anonymous, but we couldn't.

Audience:
The fact that they are veterans makes them eligible for this program. Is it available to anyone else?

Dr. Custer:
No, just veterans. Two out of three who request admission are nonveterans and have to be rejected. This will

not be the case in Maryland where they are developing a program for people in that state for both veterans and nonveterans.

Audience:

Can the gambler go back to gambling after joining Gamblers Anonymous?

Gambler A:

Well, I guess what you are asking is, not *can* we, but can we do it on a controlled basis? The answer is no. There is no such thing as control for a compulsive gambler. We cannot exercise control any more than alcoholics can who go down to 3.2 beer.

Audience:

Sort of parallel to the question that was just asked, can the pathologic gambler play games that are sometimes played for money, but just play not for money? Can they play with funny money instead of real money and not get into trouble?

Gambler A:

I would not want to play roulette with funny money. My children would not let me play Monopoly with them. There are dice in a Monopoly game. They wouldn't let me do it. We certainly tell people not to tempt, test, or tease themselves. There are so many other things to do.

Rev. Dunne:

In the AA progam we say, if you are not a lion tamer, stay out of the lion's den!

Audience:

I seem to be getting two messages. On the one hand, people say that the only effective treatment for alcoholics or gamblers is AA or GA. On the other hand I hear that we need more resources and more money. What can the rest of us do, what can professionals do?

Rev. Dunne:

It is not true that we are saying that Gamblers Anonymous is the only source of help for compulsive gamblers. We are saying that at this point there is a lack of treatment available in our municipal hospitals and in our private hospitals. We could have programs starting tomorrow if we had a million dollars. At the present time, the most effective means at our disposal in the National Council is to refer people directly to Gamblers Anonymous. We are looking for individual doctors and programs who will be willing to help us. We have a long way to go.

Audience:

Preventive medicine is a big thing these days. How do we prevent gambling? How do we work against it? Do you approve of gambling in churches?

Rev. Dunne:

I knew we were going to get to that. We have a couple of car dealers over in Jersey and they are running a raffle, they are going to raffle off a church.

This is a very, very serious problem. We have made extensive studies of the reactions of religious bodies to gambling. It is very interesting. We are aware that in the Jewish Talmud, gambling is forbidden. It is grounds for divorce. But the Talmud does allow a little gambling during the fast days to while away the time. Many of the Protestant churches abide by the so-called Protestant ethic that it is wrong to try to get money for nothing, so gambling is absolutely forbidden. This explains the ratio that Dr. Custer used regarding the various breakdowns among the faiths. The Catholic Church maintains that gambling is an indifferent act. That is, it is not morally wrong unless it is abused, if it does harm to you, your family, and so forth. So you have various backgrounds to deal with.

It is now becoming more evident among Catholic writers that the Church should take a very hard look at gambling today. In a world where only one-fifth of the people are free, where millions die of starvation every year, should we as a nation be risking millions and billions of dollars on gambling? And should we try to support a church or a religious movement with a so-called gambling operation, where the parishioners and everybody else available will come in and wager on the wheel of chance or a card game and then when they lose say, we donated to the church? Should we be in that position? It is a sad thing when churches have to exist on bingo. I get into a lot of trouble in some places when people say to me, don't bite the hand that feeds you. I couldn't in conscience today, with what I know, run a bingo without certain safeguards. It can be a social game for most people in the parish and I hope the parishioners enjoy it. But I see people come from all over the city making that bingo game night after night and heaven help you if you cancel it. If it rains in our parish or the snow comes down, the phone rings every 20 seconds. Is bingo on tonight? So it is a tremendous compulsion for some people. We have women members in GA as a result of bingo so it can be an addictive for certain people. We should look at it and evaluate it. I think that the religious question is something we can devote some serious thinking to.

Gambler A:

One thing I would like to say about preventive medicine. I have been through the school system in the State of New York and there isn't one word in any book that I have ever read that says anything about compulsive gambling. There are movies on sex, they teach about drugs and alcohol. There are lots of movies going on in the schools. There isn't one paragraph I have ever seen in a school book. Now why don't we get after our legislators to see that they at least mention it, talk about it, make it something that we can all recognize and say, here it is! Let us alert the children. Let's alert the teachers.

Dr. Custer:

This is more in secondary prevention and that is, if you have the opportunity to dissuade family members from giving a gambler a bailout, you will no doubt be able to abort the very serious continuation of the problem. Because one thing that is so consistent is the fact that once they get that bailout they are really on their way and it is very difficult to stop them at that point, until the bailout is impossible, and a prison term or something more serious, death, divorce, comes along. Many parents have approached me and I have advised, calmly I felt, that they should not give bailouts, realizing that it is a very difficult thing to do for a parent, not to bail out a child. But, I think 75 percent of them went ahead and bailed them out.

Dr. Hankoff:

I would distinguish between primary and secondary prevention. Primary, of course, is the prevention of a condition before it ever occurs or develops, and I don't think we know anything at all about the primary prevention of gambling. What we do know about primary prevention of drinking and drug use suggests that a lot of the efforts, such as educating children, seem to have a negative effect and often teaches them how to use drugs and alcohol. It is a very uncertain area. In terms of secondary prevention, I think these two suggestions and perhaps others ought to be developed; that is, to look at industry where we have a pool of individuals who are marching along the path toward pathologic gambling, or the individual who already shows the first obvious signs of needing a bailout. We perhaps might extend that to make the profile of the potential pathologic gambler better known and then develop the necessary kinds of interventions.

Gambler B:

The word "prevention" doesn't have to apply to people who haven't had the gambling problem before. I think the word prevention should include the compulsive gamblers now—the ones who have stopped, and the ones who want to stay that way. It's education, it is legislation. Why does Brecksville have a 60 percent rate of abstention? Because they have the resources, they have the money, they have the technical know-how to handle the situation. The proof of the pudding is that 60 percent of the 200 men who went through haven't gambled since. They changed their lives around.

Rev. Dunne:

We have put ads in the United Federation of Teachers paper, to get teachers interested in writing to us to get information on compulsive gambling and its prevention. We have also sent speakers to the schools; grammar schools, high schools, colleges. We will talk to any group that wants to listen. Unfortunately, we run into great problems and the prevention angle is the most difficult of all. We surveyed a high school recently and the gambling is much greater than we imagined. The gambling in a high school correlates with the alcoholism and gambling on the part of the parents, and also with child abuse. These are the people who seem to be most susceptible to gambling. We asked a group of kids in a drug installation if, while they were in high school, they were gambling and taking drugs at the same time, and the answer was yes. Even girls in the high school owed money to bookmakers and shylocks in the City of New York. So there is great work to be done among educators to try to help face the problem. We believe, as we do in alcoholism, that we can get kids on their own level to discuss it, talk about it, and deal with it with their peer group. They will take help from the peer group before they take help from us.

Gambler A:

I have received many phone calls from children who recognized the problem in their parents. When I ask them, how did you ever hear about Gamblers Anonymous, they tell me that someone came down to speak at the school.

Rev. Dunne:

We have also organized Gamateen in certain areas of the country for the children of compulsive gamblers to help them to deal with their problems with their own peer group. The worst thing I have ever seen so far is a comic book put out by the Harness Association, in which John and Judy meet this nice man who raises horses. So he brings them over to his house and asks them to bring the father along because every child should have a horse. So in the comic book they learn how trotters are trained, all the nomenclauture of the equipment, and then how to read a program. I think it is criminal that in this state children are allowed into the tracks. They are enticed into the track, particularly on Sunday with rock bands and everything else. We are creating a whole generation of gamblers. Many of them are going to be compulsive gamblers. Most of the people we have in GA started at an early age. That is what we are concerned about.

Audience:

As a school coordinator of drug and alcoholism and abuse intervention, I feel privileged to be here because I learned a great deal of factual information. But, more importantly, I developed an appreciation of an entirely new aspect of life. You can rest assured from my own part that I will take what I have learned today and put it to the best use that I can. I think I speak for everyone here when I say, to the three members of Gamblers Anonymous, from all of us, certainly the best of luck. We hope you get everything that you worked so hard to attain and that is the freedom within yourself, to be your own person.

Dr. Custer:

In closing I would like to tell you the story about the four gamblers I knew who were sitting around the table playing poker. During the game one of them suddenly dropped dead. The remaining three, out of respect for their fallen friend, decided to continue playing standing up.

REFERENCES

Cotton, C. *The complete gamester or, instructions how to play at all manner of usual and most genteel games.* Barre, Mass.: The Imprint Society, Inc., 1970 (first published, 1674).

Custer, R.L. An overview of compulsive gambling, presented at conference, *Mental Health and Industry*, South Oaks Hospital, Amityville, N.Y. April 6, 1979.

Herman, R.D. (Ed.). *Gambling*, New York: Harper and Row, 1967.

Martinez, T.M., & La Franchi, R. Why people play poker. *Transaction*, 1969, *6*, 30-52.

Oldman, D. Compulsive gamblers. *Sociological Review*, 1978, *26*:2, 349-371.

Chapter 5

OVERVIEW

Sherman N. Kieffer, M.D.*

All of the presentations these two days have been so vivid, vibrant, and timely that I feel any attempt to recapture and summarize their essence may be anticlimatic. Dr. Weisman, who began his presentation demythologizing the M.D., immediately proceeded to turn in a commanding and masterful performance which heartily supported his thesis about his own M.D.-ity. His principal thesis was that alcoholism is a "disease" with all of the trappings of such an entity. It has its own ideology; its own genetics; its own prodromata; and its own onset. He traced the course, the natural history, a treatment approach, a variety of sequelae, side effects, and all the rest that goes with a full-blown "disease." Had time allowed, certainly the "disease" versus "symptom" controversy could have been debated at length. It certainly would have come up with supporting data provided on both sides.

*Sherman N. Kieffer, M.D., is Professor and Vice-Chairman, Department of Psychiatry and Behavioral Science, School of Medicine, Health Sciences Center, State University of New York at Stony Brook. Dr. Kieffer earned his M.D. degree from the University of Minnesota and, prior to coming to Stony Brook, was the Associate Director for Patient Care, National Institute of Mental Health. Dr. Kieffer is a consultant at several hospitals, including South Oaks.

In describing and identifying factors considered under the category of "threat," since his topic title was "The Threat and the Promise," he reminded us of historical facts associated with the development of society's prejudice and the medical profession's reluctance over the years to make the diagnosis of alcoholism and to treat it not as a *symptom* of illness (my words) but as a "disease." He made a plea to the profession to make the diagnosis first, the diagnosis of primary alcoholism. "Never fail to ask frank questions about alcoholism" during routine diagnostic interviews in clinical practice was his message to the M.D.'s in the audience. While appearing to blast our profession for neglecting such a crippling and costly disease, he took consolation in the fact that recent years have seen a progressive increase in the phenomenon of acting as a "friend" to the alcoholic on the part of the establishment and an increase in the popularity of AA and self-help type of approaches. Our moral bias towards the alcoholic was counterproductive and obstructive since, he contended, the alcoholic is not responsible for his disease. He used the medical model of diabetes to make his point. Applying this type of reasoning, he felt, would go far in bringing about the long overdue change in society's attitude toward the alcoholic. Where alcoholism is associated with other behavior disorders, such as neuroses, psychoses, personality disorders, etc., he felt these had to be a *result* of rather than a *cause* of alcoholism. Again this is an issue that is too tempting to leave alone, but too controversial for discussion in the time available.

The promise for the future looked very good to Dr. Weisman from where he sat. Changes in the attitude toward alcoholism have been reflected in industry, in railroads, in the military, in the field of corrections, and above all, in the medical profession itself. He felt we are all progressive and creative and have established a note of optimism for the future. He felt that we now seem mature enough to "go out and help these people."

Dr. Weisman was followed by Dr. DuPont. Of all the statistics on drug use and drug abuse that Dr. DuPont shared with us, the most mind boggling to me, since I am from the old school, was the figure of 2 million heroin users. It so happens that I cut my proverbial psychiatric eye teeth by treating narcotic addicts, thousands of them, almost 30 years ago. In those days the number of addicts, and this was a high estimate, was around 200,000 for the entire country. Most of them were from New York City with a very few scattered around Chicago, Philadelphia, and other major metropolitan areas. They were such a minor problem to society as a whole that they formed almost no constituency. This, of course, was related to the fact that in those days it was very difficult to get the Congress to allow much money for the kind of studies in prevention, treatment, and epidemiology that have been conducted in the last decade.

Some of the factors that Dr. DuPont identified with changes in drug usage in the last decade, which he said was definitely on the increase, were staggering. Included were changes of demographic variables, economic variables and, above all, what seemed most important to him at this particular time were changes in decision making regarding life styles. He categorized the trend that drug abuse treatment might take place in the 1980s as going in four general directions.

The most important one to him was the emergence of "self-help" approaches. These approaches he looked at as a key partner in providing services to the drug abuser. In other words, the seeming success of the AA approach was too powerful and too relevant not to spread to the field of drug abuse. The recent founding of Pot Smokers Anonymous in New York is one example of this and the well-established Narcotics Anonymous is another.

A second trend was the emergence of related treatment programs for other kinds of pleasure-giving substances, such as tobacco, alcohol, marijuana, prescription drugs, tranquilizing drugs, weight control groups, exercise groups, etc. It has become part of our life style.

A third direction he related to the impact made by Betty Ford's "going public." There is now a new respectability associated with seeking treatment for dependence on pharmacologic agents. It is now socially acceptable. This he predicted will result in the mushrooming of treatment programs for the nonpoor and the nonyoung segments of our society, and will accentuate the importance of the family and other sets of close human relationships in new prevention and treatment efforts.

Last, Dr. DuPont emphasized the need for prevention programs as a co-equal of treatment programs in terms of the kind of attention and support that "prevention" must get from society. He hastened, however, to immediately qualify his prediction with the cogent recognition that, in this case, "prevention" is still doomed to the position of the proverbial equal that is somewhat "less equal than others," in this case treatment.

About the major unknown—the possibility of entirely new techniques for both prevention and treatment—he had high hopes. He shared with us a feeling of excitement, which many of us have about the current breakthroughs in the field of endorphin chemistry and its implications for our understanding and our battle with narcotic addiction. His feeling that illicit drug use in general is likely to rise is probably incontrovertible.

In support of some of his information, he shared with us the results of some of the recent NIDA surveys indicating an increase in usage rates, especially for "pot" and cocaine for those over age 30 and a growing tolerance on the part of society for occasional use of illicit drugs by adults. On the other hand, a much tougher attitude is being adopted by society toward the use of any drugs by those under 16. The use of nonlegal tactics versus drug use, such as with antismoking crusades, will also be an interesting phenomenon for a while. He expressed strong concern as a "citizen" lest our prevention and treatment programs for drug abuse become a source of erosion of our personal freedoms. Using the delicate marijuana-cocaine control controversy as a model, how compulsory should we make our therapeutic approaches? When will we resolve our struggle with the distinction between discouragement of the use of drugs and complete eradication or elimination of the use of drugs in drug abuse prevention programs? This is a dilemma in which some of us were involved 30 years ago, and I think it will be with us for some time.

The drug abuse prevention field has much to learn, Dr. DuPont felt, about the process of making life style choices and about the potentials for influencing these choices, ranging from legal incentives to economic incentives, to health insurance, and to direct intervention. The modalitites he referred to in the field of prevention included information, education, alternatives, and early intervention.

The panel meetings have been characterized by the most vibrant, active, and vivacious kind of participation that we have seen here for many years. Everybody seemed to be enthusiastic, and there was an unrestrained and meaningful exchange of a variety of points of view. The audience not only asked intelligent questions but also freely expressed their own views.

All choices, for whatever we do in life involves some kind of gamble which brings me to the presentation on gambling. We had the privilege on Friday morning of hearing probably more than many of us have heard about compulsive gambling in our lifetime, and from the points of view of both the therapist and the consumer. Certainly it was one of the best organized and substantive overviews of the problem that I have heard or read. It was presented in sufficient depth to whet our appetites for further exploration into the problem and in sufficient breadth to acquaint us with some of the parameters that I think are indispensable as we try to identify the many variables in this complex behavioral phenomenon.

In introducing his topic, Dr. Custer put gambling in its proper perspective by pointing out that it can be a pleasurable challenge for about two-thirds of the adult population who make wagers of one kind or another, but that only a small number are really "pathologic" or "compulsive" gamblers. He divided all gamblers, for the sake of discussion, into four categories. The largest group is made up of the "social gambler" who gambles for fun and over whom gambling has no control. The smallest group includes the so-called "professional gambler," who gambles solely to make money; for him, gambling is just another job. The third category includes the antisocial or criminal gambler who will steal and cheat to win. The fourth category, our subject for today, is the "compulsive" or "pathologic" gambler who gambles not only to win but to satisfy unconscious and other personal needs. Dr. Custer identifies the cardinal features of compulsive gambling as an emotional dependence on gambling, loss of control, and interference with normal functions.

Interestingly to me, he pointed out that in America we have come by some of this rightfully. The history of the United States is replete with evidence that even the 13 original colonies, along with some of their most prestigious educational institutions, were initially financed by lotteries. Attitudes toward gambling in our culture have been like the proverbial pendulum that keeps swinging between permissiveness and prohibition. Our total economic structure seems to me to be based in some degree on risks that are commonplace and highly respectable, such as stocks, bonds, futures, options, etc. We have also been inculcated with a set of values that admires a risk taker who wins and rejects the poor gambler who loses. The fact that there has been a reduction in our intolerance toward the compulsive gambler in this country, he attributes to the rise and acceptability of the AA movement that provided the framework for the start of the GA movement that began in 1957. Most of the positive social changes toward gambling began to flourish in the early 1970s with the creation of the National Commission on Compulsive Gambling, the inpatient treatment program, for which Dr. Custer has become renowned, the appointment of a Commission on the review of the national policy toward gambling, the draft of DSM-III, which included compulsive gambling as pathologic gambling and, lastly, the rapid growth of legalized gambling in the United States. In the late 1970s, pathologic gambling made the International Classification of Diseases, Ninth Edition, and more recently, the State of Maryland has allocated funds for the treatment for people with such problems. The results of the studies he shared with us indicated that the estimated $5 billion, wagered legally in the United States in 1960 grew to more than $17 billion in 1974.

The University of Michigan Group conducted a survey which revealed the statistically average, compulsive gambler, if there is such a thing, to be a white, non-Protestant, male, college graduate, under 40, with an income of over $15,000 a year. The same study group estimated that there were 1.1 million probable compulsive gamblers in this country and 3.3 million potential compulsive gamblers.

In Dr. Custer's studies of the first 100 gamblers admitted to his innovative treatment program at the Brecksville VA Medical Center, he found that nearly all compulsive gamblers have a common history of making a "big win" at some early point in their lives. He defined a "big win" as one that is equivalent to the person's annual income. The scenario he paints then proceeds from this early success that gives them the conviction that they cannot lose. They make large bets and, although they eventually lose, they may win for a while. This starts a cycle of borrowing money that they never seem able to repay. The debts eventually cause family problems, legal problems, and a great amount of stress (there were 20 suicidal attempts among the first 100 patients).

After alluding to multiple theories of causation, one may conclude that the compulsive gambler enjoys the same multifactorial etiologic status shared by those with other behavioral problems, namely that they are rooted in psychological, social, cultural, economic, and other behavioral factors. The biologic factors seem to be the only ones that are missing, but Dr. Custer says he thinks, by not too much extrapolation, one can make a case for that too. I wanted to share with him that I understand that the psychoanalysts stopped writing about the unconscious theories for compulsive gambling in the 1920s when they held their first national meeting in Las Vegas.

Dr. Custer went on to point out the similarities and differences between compulsive gambling and alcohol and drug abuse, referring to it as a drugless disorder. His description of the characteristics of the onset in the course of this disease makes one feel that it is a clinical entity that has come into its own. After sharing with us the detailed observations he made about the course, he divided the course into three major phases; namely the winning phase, the losing phase, and the desperation phase. The similarities in the description of the withdrawal syndrome of a person who suddenly ceased gambling to that of the acute withdrawal syndrome of the typical narcotic addict were striking.

I was fascinated by the presentations made by our GA representatives who shared with us highly personally tinged data about the solutions that they have found to their problems for the immediate future. Their dramatic presentations were tantamount to an in-vivo laboratory demonstration of all the important facets of this complicated "disease."

This two-day meeting was a most useful forum for the discussion and exploration of the differences as well as the commonalities of three important distinctive addictive disorders that, unfortunately, have been on the increase over the past decade. I hope that the group sessions and workshops of both afternoons will generate new ideas that we might apply to our efforts in stemming the tide of these trends whether in industry or for society as a whole.

INDEX